Holden's Ghosts

The Life and Times of Sir Isaac Holden:
Inventor, Woolcomber and
Nonconformist Radical Liberal M.P.

Tony Holden

Published by Leen Editions

ISBN 978-0-9931612-1-6

Holden's Ghosts - The Life and Times of Sir Isaac Holden: Inventor, Woolcomber and Nonconformist Radical Liberal M.P.

Copyright © Tony Holden 2015

Published: 2015

The right of Tony Holden to be identified as author of this Work has been asserted by him in accordance with sections 77 and 78 of the Copyright, Designs and Patents Act 1988.

All rights reserved. No part of this publication may be reproduced, stored in retrieval system, copied in any form or by any means, electronic, mechanical, photocopying, recording or otherwise transmitted without written permission from the publisher. You must not circulate this book in any format.

Contents

Acknowledgements	5
Preface	7
1. Introduction	10
2. Joseph in the House of Pharaoh	17
3. Take a place out of town.	24
4. The Search for a Prudent Wife	29
5. New Beginnings.	41
6. Cité Anglaise	60
7. Isaac Holden et Fils	69
8. New Alliances	75
Photographs relating to Isaac Holden.	83
9. Dissenters Grievances	102
10. All for Glory: the Franco-Prussian War	125
11. Return to the fray: infidels and secularists, and spoliators	134
12. The Phoenix Park murders and a return to parliament	148
13. For fear of saying hard things	159
14. Health & Longevity, a Baronetcy and a Strike	167
15. Death Duties and Isaac's last session in Parliament	176
Endnotes	188
Sources	192
Index	213

Acknowledgements

I am very grateful to Alison Cullingford, Special Collections Librarian and her Assistant, Martin Levy, at the J.B. Priestley Library at Bradford University for the warm and friendly help and advice they have given me in my research for this book. I am also grateful to them and the university for allowing me to use some of the images in the collection in this publication. I would also like to thank the staff in the Special Collections at the Brotherton Library at Leeds University.

I am grateful to the staff at Bradford Industrial Museum for explaining the workings of the Square Motion comb and allowing me to use its image.

I would like to thank Damien Aked for all his helpful advice and detailed work in editing, preparing and illustrating the publication ready for publication and Sue Aked for her work in preparing the family tree at the end of the book.

I would like to thank Justin Pearce-Neudorf for his help in formatting and laying out the book ready for publication.

Thanks also go to my readers Ken Bayliss, Bert Clough, Pamela Gant and Joe Holden and for commenting on earlier drafts.

Preface

At the end of a life spanning almost the whole of the nineteenth century, Isaac Holden was described as 'one of the most notable examples of a self-made man'. Radicalised by his early experience of being brought up in dire poverty, he was one of the northern nonconformist entrepreneurs who found his home in the radical wing of the Liberal Party. He had been dismissed as a young teacher for his nonconformist views. Entering into the wool trade he discovered a passion for experimentation and technological innovation and went on to play a major role in developing the Square Motion wool-combing machine. Overcoming the stigma of an early business failure in Bradford and struggling with the loss of his first wife, he set out to make his fortune by starting a wool combing business in revolutionary France in 1848 in what was to prove to be a rancorous partnership with Samuel Cunliffe Lister. Gaining sole control of the business ten years later, Isaac then expanded into Bradford in the 1860s. By perfecting the square motion comb and buying up the patent rights to opposing machines he became the largest wool comber in the world. This was at a time in which the woollen and worsted industries were a major part of the British economy representing around 10 per cent of national income and employing around a quarter of a million people.

First entering into parliament in 1865 and serving as an MP with a number of interludes until 1895, he worked for the final abolition of slavery, electoral reform, Irish Home Rule, and church disestablishment. Lauded in his obituaries as Bradford's "Grand Old Man", he was depicted in the press as a frugal man who lived a simple life. However his old partner Lister, who had become Lord Masham, wrote a vituperative letter to the Editor of The Engineer responding to its obituary:

> 'At last that wonderful man, Sir Isaac Holden, has joined the great majority and the story of his life is now before the public and it seems a pity to spoil so pleasant and entertaining story as that given to us by the public press… But biography to be worth anything should give us facts, and not fiction, although it might not be so amusing'.

After reading at the start of my research for this biography the highly edited, 'Holden Illingworth Letters', published by Isaac's grandson in the 1920s, I worked my way through the extensive archives which contain Isaac's personal, business and political papers in the Special Collections at the J.B. Priestley Library at Bradford University and the Brotherton Library at Leeds University. As the facts of Isaac's life emerged from the archives I soon discovered that Isaac, like many of the eminent Victorians with whom he was associated, was a man of contradictions and conflicts in his personal, business and political life. Although supporting radical causes, as a capitalist and rugged individualist he was opposed to most factory reform. Purporting to avow equality of treatment between sons and daughters, he was deeply patriarchal; one of his daughters was an early suffragette who was willing to challenge the authority of her father when her own interest was threatened. His sons and nephews played key roles in his business life, but his less than partial treatment of them led to a rivalry for his approval. Health-obsessed and a supporter of the temperance movement, he laid in a fine wine cellar at his mansion at Oakworth and was an inveterate cigar smoker. Personally brave, Isaac was a gregarious man with a wry sense of humour. Loyal and generous to family and friends, his large-scale philanthropy was nevertheless guided, not only by moral principle, but enlightened self-interest.

I discovered that when his great grandson, Sir Edward Holden, donated the papers to the two university archives he had withheld the letters Isaac exchanged in his two-year courtship of his second wife, Sarah Sugden. These letters reveal not only the contortions and manipulations he was prepared to go through to secure Sarah's hand, but also her quiet self-assertiveness and calm assurance in seeking a marriage of equals.

Many other characters also revealed themselves in my trawl through the archives: his domineering partner, Samuel Cunliffe Lister, and Lister's duplicitous French agent, Ferdinand Tavernier, his strident son-in-law and fellow radical Liberal MP, Alfred Illingworth and other Liberal politicians including John Bright, W.E. Forster, Gladstone, Edward Miall, and John Morley, the trade union leader, Tom Mann, and the Labour leader, Kier Hardie. Tales of bravery emerged like that shown by his nephew, Jonathan Holden, during the Franco-Prussian War, and of the fortitude of the workers in the woollen industry who built lives for themselves and their families despite the intense deprivation of the newly industrialised towns in both France and England.

1. Introduction

In 1807, the year Isaac Holden was born in a tiny thatched cottage in Hurlet, a mining village near Paisley, the Napoleonic Wars had been going on for seven years and still had six more to run. The ending of the Napoleonic Wars was followed by considerable hardship exacerbated by the introduction of the Corn Laws in 1815, which kept food prices high at a time of declining wages.

'A Man's a Man for A' That'

Radical ideas took a strong hold particularly in the weaving communities in the central belt of Scotland. In April 1820 60,000 workers from the weaving communities across the central belt of Scotland came out on strike. When the mill workers in his hometown of Johnstone joined the strike, 13-year-old Isaac Holden learnt that his schoolmaster, John Fraser, had been arrested. Fraser, "the Old Radical", railed at that time against: 'the Corn Laws, the petitions of the State clergy to retain them in the face of high priced food.' Fraser was eventually released after four months of imprisonment but others were less fortunate, three leaders of the failed revolt were executed by hanging and then decapitated, and eighteen others were sentenced to penal transportation.

John Fraser had previously been dismissed from a job as an excise officer for reciting Robbie Burns, A Man's a Man for A' That, a song influenced by Tom Paine's, The Rights of Man. Unrepentant,

Fraser had the words of the song printed for the boys in his school to learn by heart:

A prince can mak a belted knight,

A marquis, duke, an' a' that;

But an honest man's abon his might,

Gude faith, he maunna fa' that!

For a' that, an' a' that,

Their dignities an' a' that;

The pith o' sense, an' pride o' worth

Robbie Burns (1795), Is There for Honest Poverty (or A Man's a Man for A' That)

Fraser said prophetically to Isaac when he left the school, 'he hoped hereafter he would gladly incur dismissal for any good cause'. Fraser went on to found the Chartist newspaper, The True Scotsman.

'A puny little unthriving child, too feeble to go to school in winter', Isaac attributed his small stature to the hard times in which his childhood was cast. His father was a farmer and lead miner in Cumbria. When the landlord of his father's smallholding at Nenthead near Alston in Cumbria doubled the rent in 1780, he moved to Scotland and worked as coal miner; when work fell off at one pit he moved his family on to the next. A strong believer in education, his father played a leading role in setting up the local village school Isaac attended in Hurlet until the family moved to Kilbarchan in 1812. After a short stint at grammar school, 11-year-old Isaac was engaged as a drawboy to two hand weavers. At his father's insist-

ence, he attended night school and on his days off spent his time at a nearby joiner's shop. Two years later, the family moved on to Johnstone and a brief improvement in family fortunes enabled Isaac to go to Fraser's school.

When he was 15, the family moved on again to Paisley where Isaac was apprenticed for a year as a shawl weaver to one of his mother's relatives. He returned the following year to a school run by "Citizen" John Kennedy, another prominent radical republican. Graduating from pupil to assistant teacher, Isaac remained at Kennedy's school until he was twenty. He later spoke about Kennedy and Fraser as being:

> 'Two of the most distinguished radicals of the time ...
> Not only did he imbibe his Radicalism from these men,
> but a very high class of education for the use of which
> providence destined him in after life'.

His mother, *'a pious, industrious, high-principled Scotchwoman'*, desperately wanted him to become a Methodist minister. He was chosen for itinerant Wesleyan mission work, but found that his health was not up to the task. When Isaac was nineteen, his father died leaving his mother and younger brother, George, dependent upon him. He continued to support George in various ways, mostly by bailing him out when he got into financial difficulties, throughout his life. Around this time he fell in love with sixteen-year-old Marion Love, described by his mother as 'quite blithe and hauty like'. When he moved south to Leeds one of his friends, a local preacher from Paisley, became their go-between. In this way Isaac conducted a semi-clandestine five-year courtship of Marion by letter, including a love poem written by him:

> *'I see no beauty in the shining day*
>
> *But peak in loneliness and pine away*

Wrapt in the past mine ardent longing flee

To dwell with thee'

Dismissal for any good cause

Two further experiences helped to shape the radical stance Isaac was to adopt in his later political life towards schisms within the Methodist church, which he deplored, and abuses of power by the established Church of England and the landed aristocracy.

He started a teaching post at the Queens Street Academy in Leeds in January 1828, but his stay was to be short lived. The head teacher, Mr. Sigston, a strict Methodist, was expelled from the Wesleyan Society in Leeds when he objected to the installation of an organ in the chapel on the grounds that playing organ music in church was the work 'of the devil'. Sigston left to found a new church, the Protestant Methodists, and asked Isaac to join him. Isaac refused to do so and was summarily dismissed by the dogmatic Sigston from his teaching post.

He moved on to teach at Lingards Free School in Slaithwaite, which formed part of the Earl of Dartmouth's estates. Isaac continued preaching on Sundays and after a few months the head teacher, Mr Butterfield, told him that the Church of England vicar of Slaithwaite threatened to inform the school's patron, the Earl of Dartmouth, unless he got rid of "that Methodist". Butterfield told Isaac, 'he was prepared to incur the displeasure of the patron rather than part with me; but I told him that could not allow him to suffer any injury on my account, so I left Slaithwaite'.

The Lucifer match

After these two early set backs, Isaac taught Classics and Chemistry at the Castle Street Academy in Reading at a salary of £20 per annum, out of which he sent regular remittances to his mother in Paisley. It is whilst teaching in Reading that Isaac claimed to have invented the 'Lucifer match'. He later explained in evidence he gave to the Patents Committee of the House of Commons in 1871 how he and other chemistry teachers of the time had demonstrated Sir Humphrey Davy's explosive compound by adding gum arabic made of hardened sap taken from two species of the acacia tree to stabilise it. Davy had lost an eye whilst experimenting with the compound in its free state. In the classic chemistry demonstration the compound causing the explosion was attached to a small splinter of wood, but the speed of the reaction was generally too quick for the wood to ignite. After conducting his own experiments in 1829, Isaac solved the problem by interposing a layer of sulphur between the wood spelks or splinters and the explosive material to improve the reliability and safety of ignition.

The headmaster, Mr Greathead, suggested that a friend, Samuel Jones, a Chemist at Light House in London, might provide the capital to take out a patent on his invention. Declining the offer, Isaac gave Samuel Jones the right to manufacture the matches, which he marketed as 'Lucifer matches'. However, white phosphorous matches developed by the Frenchman, Charles Sauria, quickly superseded these early Lucifers.

In his evidence to the Patents Committee, Isaac contrasted his unwillingness to patent an invention which 'were but a happy thought without an expenditure of time and money to mature' with the need for patent protection for those that came about as a result of a great deal of work and expense. His claims to have invented the

Lucifer match were later contested in correspondence in the 1890s between Isaac and John Parrott, who was spearheading a committee campaigning to have a memorial erected in Stockton on Tees for the deceased John Walker as the inventor of the Lucifer match. The courteous correspondence made it clear that, whilst the inventions were independent of one another, Walker's had preceded Isaac's by two years. Isaac's addition of sulphur had nevertheless been an improvement. Presented with the evidence he conceded to Walker's claim, and was graciously invited by John Parrott to become a vice president of the Promoters of the Walker Memorial Fund.

Moving back to Glasgow in April 1830, Isaac advertised night classes for: 'Young Gentleman engaged in the Counting House during the day, and others wishing to acquire a free and elegant Business-hand or a thorough knowledge of Arithmetic, Accounts and Practical Bookkeeping.' The venture was short-lived as he was offered a job later as a bookkeeper on a salary of £100 per year in the worsted mill of Townsend Bros in Cullingworth near Bingley in the West Riding. He travelled to Cullingworth on the newly opened Liverpool to Manchester railway in November 1830 and was to remain with Townsend Bros for 16 years; the Townsends were fellow Wesleyans.

Marriage and children

In the spring of 1831 Isaac wrote to Marion's parents requesting their permission to marry, concealing his clandestine courtship of her but admitting as he did so, 'It is now five years since my more intimate acquaintance with her, which you may have considered too soon to form such an intimacy, but this you must excuse as I mistook Marion's age and my attachment by that time had accumulated to an almost invincible force.' Permission granted, they were married in Paisley on 10th April 1832.

Tragically Marion's mother and sister both died on the same day later that year in a cholera outbreak in Paisley in which around 450 people died. The town subsequently suffered devastating levels of unemployment. His father-in-law, Angus Love, wrote telling him, 'Several hundreds of men are daily employed breaking up stones in quarry, single men get sixpence, married men with 2 children nine pence and those with three children 1/- per day where it not for this many would before this no doubt have died for want.' Angus Love remained a regular correspondent and loyal confidante to Isaac.

Isaac and Marion's home was often a place of refuge for Scots moving south in search of work and others who had fallen on hard times locally. The following year Marion's seven-year-old sister, Jessie, came to live with them and their first son, Angus, was born. A second son, Edward, was born in 1835 and his growing family was to be completed with the birth of two daughters, Mary in 1838 and Margaret two years later.

Playing a leading role in the local Methodist community, Isaac travelled on horseback or on foot to preach at local chapels in the Bingley circuit on Sundays. When he learnt that the local vicar had sequestrated land to build a Church of England school, he followed his father's example and successfully campaigned to have an independent Wesleyan school built near to Townsend's mill. The episode strengthened his loathing for the power of the Church of England and he wrote to his old mentor, John Kennedy, advocating the formation of 'an association among private members of our body [of Wesleyans] in opposition to the State Church.'

2. Joseph in the House of Pharaoh

The ethics of mechanisation

Townsends was the first maker of worsted heald yarns in the Bradford district and the main source of employment in Cullingworth, at its peak employing 800 workers. The combing of long wool, to remove the 'noils' or short fibres and separate them from the longer fibres to make 'tops', was still done by hand.

When Robert Townsend took him to see a hand comber at work Isaac asked if the operation had been attempted by machine. He was told that many attempts had been made but that that every trial had failed.

At the same time Isaac had doubts about the morality of mechanisation and the consequences for hand combers. The Wool Combers Union was very active in trying to protect the interests of the skilled hand combers who, renowned for their pugnacity, resisted mechanisation in every way they could. There had been a large-scale hand combers strike in Bradford and Leeds in 1825, which had lasted 22 weeks, and there was a wool combers strike in 1832.

Isaac sought the advice of his old school master, John Kennedy, on the dilemma. Kennedy wrote advising:

> *"I conceive you to be bound to obtain before proceeding to construct such machinery, strong probable evidence for*

believing that its employment would at no very remote period be productive of such good to society at large and especially the labouring poor as could more than compensate for the immediate evil occasioned to those whom its introduction might deprive of bread."

Within four years Isaac graduated from the role of bookkeeper to manager and was sent to represent the firm at the Paris Exhibition in 1834. He first saw the mechanised Collier combing machine working at the Exhibition and successfully persuaded Townsends to introduce it into the factory.

Taking Kennedy's advice about the need for empirical evidence of the advantages of mechanisation Isaac conducted his own trials comparing the work of 47 hand combers with work done by machine. He produced a cost benefit analysis, which showed that at this early stage of mechanisation the benefits were marginal. His early notebooks show that as early as 1833-1835 he began to be preoccupied with making technical improvements to the combing process. Mechanisation brought about the end of hand combing; Henry Ripley, who was to become one of Isaac's political rivals, later estimated that a fully developed machine comb could produce the output of 100 hand combers.

Corn Laws and idle Bishops

The Corn Law (Importation Act 1815) introduced after the Napoleonic Wars provided a high duty on foreign corn based on a sliding scale, affording protection for the landed farmers but acting against the interest of the poorer consumer. Agitation for the reform of the Corn Laws, which increased after the failed harvest and industrial depression of 1836, reached its height in the early 1840s and did not pass Isaac idly by. He was active in Richard Cobden and John Bright's Anti-Corn Law cause. Cobden and Bright shared Isaac's northern manufacturing background. Richard Cobden, the leader of the Anti-corn Law League and renowned campaigner for Free Trade, was the successful owner of a calico-printing factory in Manchester. John Bright, who became one of the leading radical Liberal MPs of his generation, was a Quaker whose father had started the Greenbank cotton-spinning mill and became the second largest employer in Rochdale. Isaac wrote to the Editor of *The Sun* and to the chairman of the Anti-Corn Law League calling on the League to 'address themselves to actions not words, to devise and act on some practical measure to relieve the nation from the hellish incubus, which oppresses it.'

He set out a plan calling for the formation of a joint stock Corn Trading Company in order to provide foreign corn to the members of the League. Interestingly, Isaac supported the middle-class-led Anti-Corn Law League, but not the working-class-led Chartists who called for immediate parliamentary reform and whom his old mentor, John Fraser, played a significant role supporting in Scotland

He also wrote to the Editor of *The Sun* attacking Peel's Tory Government for supporting a system of National Schools, which would in effect be run by the Church of England, writing that such a system 'would be communicated by the idle Bishops, whose lessons would resemble their sermons preached in our national churches, of which it has been well said "that their apparent object is to keep the people's mind from thinking"'. He proposed that the government establish a system of non-sectarian teacher training schools.

In 1846, he sent his own two sons (then aged 13 and 11) to the Wesley College near Sheffield from where the headmaster, Mr.

Waddy, wrote informing him that Angus had been subjected to a "pillowing", but the culprit had been moved to another room.

The House of Pharaoh

As his contribution to the business in Cullingworth grew Isaac made repeated requests to the Townsend brothers for an increased share of the profits and then for a partnership. In response to one such request for a 7.5 per cent share of the profits made at the end of 1837, Robert Townsend likened Isaac to 'Joseph in the House of Pharaoh'. The request was acceded to and his salary rose to £200 per annum. From 1838 onwards he began to plan for and, by living frugally, managed to save capital to set up his own business. The relationship with his employers had begun to turn sour and the brothers proposed to reduce his share of the profits to 5 per cent, complaining of lapses in his time keeping and of allowing part of the yarn to be split.

'Require them to apologise for the unmerited charges and the degradation of employing someone to watch my attendance at the mills. If they are indifferent about my staying and not willing to place me in a more honorable and advantageous position - resign', he wrote in his notebook in 1842. They agreed to pay him six per cent, so he was being paid £500 a year by the time he left the firm four years later at the age of 39 years.

One of the sources of his frustration at Townsends was the brothers' reluctance to apply for patents; 'indiscriminate anti patent principle may lead to our separation', he wrote in his notebook after one meeting with them. Keen to establish his reputation as an inventor his notebooks are full of ideas for patents and by 1843 he had begun to draft these up in his own name and to have them countersigned by colleagues. He also recorded a visit he had made to see a new combing machine that Samuel Cunliffe Lister and Donnisthorpe were making, which he felt was too complicated, 'Could put Lister and Donnisthorpe right would they give us the machines and then work them ourselves… they are on the right principle … though they are inferior to Collier.'

The stress of his relationship with the Townsends was beginning to take its toll on his marriage. Unwell, Marion took a short break in Harrogate from where she wrote to him on June 17th 1845:

> 'I don't feel right unless I am always thinking about you and home … I console myself with the thought that some day or other we shall have the pleasure of spending a fortnight together at Harrogate. I believe we never shall if we remain in our present situation. You see we are very much overlooked by others …I think if our income was smaller than it is we should be better off of ourselves and then we might go away here without anyone to find fault – what is our life to be under such misery.'

In 1846 Isaac finally broke with the Townsends. The split seems to have been reasonably amicable. Robert Townsend's daughter, Eliza, became Isaac's ward when her father died. He took this responsibility seriously and was also the executor of her estate.

He rented a mill at Pit Lane in Bradford for £210 per year and began to make Paisley Shawl 'middles'. Paisley shawls were fashionable accessories in the 1840s. Bradford, known as 'Worstedoplis', was fast becoming the international centre of the worsted trade. Worsted is made from smooth compactly spun yarn. Long fibered wool is combed and spun using an average to hard twist in the spinning. The fabric is napless and tightly woven. Bradford's growth accelerated with the production of mixed worsteds, which combined alpaca and mohair with other wools to manufacture cheaper worsted cloths, able to compete with Lancashire's cotton goods.

At that time the fastest growing town in England, Bradford was enveloped in thick smog pouring from more that a hundred mill chimneys. The average age of death in Bradford in 1840 was just 18.7 years and half of all babies died before they were 5 years old. The Bradford Woolcombers' Report compiled and produced by woolworkers in 1845 demonstrated a massive degree of overcrowding with more than seven people commonly sharing a back-to-back, two-roomed house, which would generally lack a kitchen or toilet. There was no proper sewerage system so household and manufacturers' effluent were both discharging into Bradford Beck, which fed into the canal causing a build up of noxious gases with 'the flame flickering on the surface where gas was bubbling out.'

This was far from being a propitious time to start a new business. In 1846, the first signs of a deep depression began to appear to be followed a year later by a financial collapse triggered by railway speculation and a crash on the Stock Exchange. Isaac's business experienced financial problems from the start and the Bradford Bank, from whom he had loaned capital, and his landlord both harried him. Despite these difficulties Isaac also indulged in railway speculation buying small amounts of shares in three companies. The business closed in less than two years.

Isaac narrowly escaped the social stain of becoming bankrupt. He was left with considerable debts including to James Mitchell for £795, the bank in Bradford £496 and the Hall Commercial Banking Company for £160. Some of his debts were not paid off for years; one loan of £350 made by William Jessop was not paid off until 1853.

Isaac's beloved wife Marion became seriously ill in 1846 and she died of tuberculosis on 7th April 1847. 'She died in the full triumph of the Faith', Isaac wrote to a friend. He made a plaintive entry into his notebook, 'paid Betty Ackroyd £1 for attending to my poor late wife'. He was now left a desolate widower with four children to care for. He withdrew his sons from the Wesleyan Grammar School in Sheffield. Fourteen year-old Angus started working in his father's office and Edward was sent to a local school. His daughters were educated at home.

3. Take a place out of town.

A photograph of Isaac taken at around that time shows a small, self-assured bearded man with a strong and intense gaze. He is clothed in frock coat, and waistcoat and silk bow tie. In this image his strikingly sparkling eyes appear to be looking intently into the future.

Having long hankered for full recognition for his own technical innovations, he began discussions with Samuel Cunliffe Lister in the summer of 1845 about developing a 'carding' patent. 'Carding' is a mechanical process that takes place before combing wool; carding machines use rollers to disentangle and mix wool fibres to produce a continuous web or sliver of worsted yarns suitable for subsequent processing as worsted cloth.

Samuel Cunliffe Lister and Isaac were from widely divergent backgrounds. Eight years younger than Isaac, Lister was born on December 31st 1815 at Calverley Hall near Leeds. He was the son of Ellis Cunliffe Lister, an Anglican Liberal, elected as the first Member of Parliament for Bradford after the 1832 Reform Act. His father had married the heiress of the Lister's of Manningham, changing his name to Cunliffe-Lister, and inherited the Lister fortune. Privately educated at a school in London on Clapham Common, Samuel Cunliffe Lister was being trained for entering the church (his grandmother had bequeathed him the Rectory of Addingham), but he did not pursue this vocation. His first job, which lasted a year, was in the counting house of Sands, Turner & Co in Liverpool. In 1833 he became a sales representative for his elder brother, John, who spun yarn for making shawls at his Red Beck mill in Shipley. In this role he made several voyages to the United States earning him the nickname 'American Sam'. In 1837, at the age of 23 he went into business with his brother, John, in the worsted-spinning mill their father had newly built for them at Manningham. He took James Ambler in as a business partner when his brother retired in 1845. Lister showed considerable technical acumen and quickly saw the commercial advantages of patenting his innovations; with more than 150 patents to his name he was said to have patented more inventions than any man in England.

Hard working and intensely competitive, Lister was very strategic in his business outlook. He quickly saw that it was in his long-term interest to purchase competitors' innovations in order to secure a monopoly of the new technology and bought a half share in George Edmund Donnisthorpe's wool combing patent in 1842. Based in Leicester George Donnisthorpe had patented minor improvements to current wool combing machines in the 1830s but made a larger advance in 1842 that he patented. Lister contracted Donnisthorpe and formed a partnership to assist him in developing further improvements, which Lister then patented in his own name between 1844 and 1848; further patents were taken out in their joint names in 1849 and 1850. The 'Nip' machine wool combing machine, in which the tuft of wool was drawn by a 'nipper' [a pair of curved metal jaws] through a gill comb, was to be the key product of Lister and Donnisthorpe's combined investigations. Lister bought out Donnisthorpe's initial Nip patent in 1851. [The Frenchman, Heilmann, had also separately patented the principle of a 'nip' comb in France.] The introduction of the Nip comb had a dramatic impact upon Bradford's hand combers, whose numbers fell by an estimated 10,000 within five years.

Isaac and Lister's discussions took place behind Donnisthorpe's back to safeguard against him taking a rival patent. In the summer of 1847, they signed a Memorandum of Agreement about taking out a joint patent, 'For carding combing and spinning wool'. They now began to collaborate in the development of the Square Motion combing machine, the original idea of which was to be the source of a bitter life long dispute between them. Lister applied for a patent for the Square Motion machine in 1848; although Isaac had drafted the technical specifications for the patent, it was taken out in Lister's name. (At this point Isaac used the patent application to write to Townsends suggesting that if they were to offer him a full partnership he would not pursue his proposed partnership with Lister. There is no record of their response.)

Probably as early as 1846 Lister and Isaac began to forge the idea of setting up a joint enterprise in France; Isaac's notebooks show him purchasing French language textbooks that year. He already had some familiarity with the French woollen trade and had a passport dated 26th April 1834 from when he visited the Paris Exhibition on behalf of Townsends. France had market dominance in higher priced, all wool worsted cloths and it had recently become possible for foreign investors to take a French patent, which Lister first did in 1843. For his part Lister was determined to forge a partnership that would enable him to extend his patenting acquisition strategy and to exercise a wool combing monopoly in both England and France. Isaac on the other hand saw it as an opportunity to use the capital provided by Lister to perfect the Square Motion machine, which was well suited to the fine merino wool used in the French worsted industry, and see off the competition by producing the best combed wool on the market. As Katrina Honeyman and Jordan Goodman have shown in their book, 'Technology and Enterprise: Isaac Holden and the Mechanisation of Woolcombing in France 1848-1914', the conflicting aims of the two partners were to drive the two men apart as they pursued their own strategic objectives.

Enter the bewigged Tavernier

Leaving his brother George to wind up his affairs in Bradford, Isaac travelled to France in September 1848 with Ferdinand Tavernier, Lister's French agent, in search of suitable premises to locate the factory. Tavernier was retained by the Lister Holden partnership, his main role being to sell the firm's commission combing services, but as Lister's agent he was required by him to keep a covert eye on Isaac's financial management and expenditure. This placed him in direct conflict with Isaac. Thriving on intrigue Tavernier was to prove to be unscrupulous in playing one partner off against the other whenever it suited his interest to do so.

Tavernier was engaged to marry Donnisthorpe's sister and kept in close touch with his future brother in law who also harboured designs on setting up a business in France. The 'bewigged' Tavernier was closely allied to one of France's leading worsted manufacturers, Baron de Fourment, who gave initial advice but was later to become a deadly rival.

The year 1848 was one of political upheaval that started in France and quickly spread to Germany, Poland, Italy, and the Austro-Hungarian Empire. When Isaac arrived in September, France was still in turmoil following the Revolution that in February had seen the overthrow of Louis Philippe as King of France, followed by the declaration of a Republic and the notorious June days of 'civil war' in Paris. On 17th September 1848, whilst Isaac was in Paris,

Louis Napoleon Bonaparte was elected Deputy for Paris and by December he had been elected President of the Republic.

Lister wrote advising Isaac, 'if you can take a place out of town it would be better… less likely to let out your modus vivandi which I think is of great consequence as your keeping exclusive possession of your trade will depend as much on keeping your machines secret, as upon the patent.' They found a site south of Paris but this was not to be pursued.

On Isaac's return from France the partnership deed with Lister was finalised. Isaac was to manage the firm in France with a minimum salary of £200 (tied to profits) and his initial capital outlay was set at £300. Lister was to provide his patented combing machines and the remaining capital, on which he would receive five per cent interest per annum. Their focus was on 'commission combing', a process in which the worsted spinner customer provides the raw wool which the comber then processes and separates the long from the short wool - the 'top' from the 'noil'. However within a month of signing their partnership agreement Lister was writing to Isaac announcing that he was reducing his initial capital outlay from £3000 to £2000 and suggesting that the proportion of the profits should be divided in the proportion of two to one in Lister's favour. Isaac resisted this proposal but it was enacted the following year, Lister mockingly wrote, *'You are a lucky man to have the chance of a third of such a business.'*

4. The Search for a Prudent Wife

Whilst he was starting up the new business in France, the newly widowed Isaac began to look for a new wife. His turbulent courtship of Sarah Sugden, a deceased spinning mill owner's daughter and fellow member of the Eastbrook Methodist Chapel in Bradford, was almost entirely conducted by a correspondence spanning the period May 1848 to March 1850.

The 'courtship letters' were kept separately from the archived correspondence initially collated for use in the Holden Illingworth Letters privately published by Isaac's grandson, Eustace Illingworth, in 1927 and are still in the possession of the family. They tell their own story and reveal much about Isaac's state of mind following Marion's death, his deeply patriarchal attitudes and expectations of a 'prudent wife'. They show that in matters of the heart Isaac could be economical with the truth. Sarah Sugden was forthright in tackling Isaac about the inconsistencies in the way in which he portrayed his departure from Bradford and in her determination to be treated, not as the "weaker vessel", but as a partner in marriage. Isaac had first met her in his Cullingworth days when she was keeping house for her brothers in nearby Oakworth.

Their courtship correspondence begins with a letter sent by Sarah on May 23 1848 in which she refers to a letter from him:

> *'Having no inclination to keep your mind in suspense and perplexed I take up my pen at the earliest opportunity. I*

> *cannot tell what to say more than I have said…your last visit …impressed on my mind the necessity of firmness… …I have not forbid you coming to the house as a christian friend ….I trust we shall part friends. No condemnation dwell in the breast of one towards the other. With no feelings contrary to christian love'.*

When Isaac wrote asking permission to visit again she responded unpromisingly:

> *'Now I am fully convinced it will not do for you to come again as the thing is so painful as it may lie. I see nothing less than violence will do and I am resolved that I will not again receive a visit from you and that you will not give yourself the pain of making the attempt'.*

Just before his departure for France Isaac wrote a letter from his home in Bradford proposing marriage (and again in October and November) only to be met with requests from Sarah for time to consider. He wrote in exaggerated terms at the end of November setting out the case for her marrying him:

> '1st *The religious, which is the most important. In order to do good to the world we cannot I believe do it more effectively than in France… especially considering that I shall have a position of influence with the French Government….*
>
> 2nd *The personal – these must be known to you. Thank God I trust my character and principles are unchanged from what they ever have been. I still enjoy the confidence and affection of my Christian Brethren.*

> 3rd As to temporal matters ... my future income, as far as human things are so, will be certain; and I believe so large as to give me the power of doing much good to the world, as well as to ourselves'.

Some good ladies have had their hands in the pie

Isaac assumed the marriage was going ahead but she had heard rumours and wrote to him again in March 1849 challenging him:

> 'to be open and honest with each other... I have been informed of your asserting you were going to marry in April & along with the person you were marrying you was taking such a sum of money. Also I am told you have a very small share in your concern & you are a person giving colour in imagination more than reality.... As I have begun to speak I will venture to mention another, the remarks by some in Bradford suppose that you have lost most of your money. I heard speak of one influential person in the Eastbrook Society saying he hoped I should never fall into your hands'.

Rattled by the rumour mill back home Isaac wrote:

> '16 April 1849, Paris, ... I find some good ladies have had their hands in the pie who had used certain arts and efforts to gain my kindly attention.... One of the ladies has been very industrious in putting suggestions into a channel, which they certainly intended would produce a prejudicial effect'.

Friends say whatever you do, don't go to France

Her brother, Jonas, who was advising Sarah, was worried about the upheavals in France. Sarah's letter of 8th June reflects their concerns:

> 'I have at last received your long looked for letter. Please pardon the jest when I ask if you cannot find time to write, how will you find time to marry? Since I wrote last Bro Jonas has given intimation of his intention to visit France… I think he still has his fears respecting France and risk in your adventure in business there. There appears little confidence in it as a nation…. friends say whatever you do, don't go to France'.

Five days later on 13th June 1849 14,000 leftists marched on the Elysées Palace in Paris and were attacked by cavalry who dispersed them. In the evening, the National Assembly declared a state of siege at the request of President Louis Bonaparte. Isaac played down the true state of affairs in France:

> '16th June 1849, There have been these four days a little excitement in Paris but it was nothing. I was in the heart of it everyday, but it did not divert me from business. I saw nearly all and am astonished at the papers making so much of it'

The surgeon's delicate probe

Isaac's next letter takes a dramatic turn; the letter from Sarah to which it refers has been lost, but it seems to have repeated local gossip that Isaac had previously proposed to two other women before proposing to Sarah:

> 'Paris, 6 July 1849 I do not at all remember what I may have said to you before … I think you must have misunderstood me altogether in reference to Mrs C. I was much teased about by Mrs C by several parties, perhaps because she had always been very kind to my children and had been intimate with my late wife; and I confess that it had influenced my mind a little… my thoughts never had expression in acts or words. I never spoke such a thing to Mrs C nor authorised any one to make any proposal from me to her on the subject. I am not aware of having made any proposal of any kind, even the most distant to any lady or female of any rank, except in the case of my blunder to Miss R and then to you yourself. That is clearly only two cases'.

Aware that the rumour mill back in Bradford was still running against him, Isaac wrote again on 12th July in a more provocative tone:

> I hope you will not listen to those friends who recommend so protracted a postponement of our union.... should the slightest hesitation on your part my dear Sarah or such serious objections on the part of your family as to control your decision, I should much rather place you at perfect liberty, and relieve you from every obligation in our correspondence.

Sarah's response was pained:

> 'There was a remark that went as a dagger to my heart… nor had I in the least calculated of such a remark as placing at perfect liberty, it felt to cut rather deep…I was

not aware of giving you the impression of indecision ... or any objection in the family'.

Isaac wrote asking her to:

'Be assured they were only intended to act as the surgeon's delicate probe ... I am now assured of your firm and decided affection'.

The Weaker Vessel?

Jonas wanted to protect Sarah's inheritance from passing to Isaac on their marriage and for this to be enshrined in a Marriage Settlement. In 19th Century England a man by taking a wife essentially laid claim to her and to all her assets.

As a matter of common law her dowry and everything she possessed at the time of the marriage (or earned later) belonged to her husband. Marriage Settlements circumvented this problem by setting up a trust for the wife guaranteeing her access to specified funds during her husband's life and after his death.

In the patriarchal system it was the older brother, Jonas, not the sister who led the negotiations for a Marriage Settlement. Sarah dutifully passed on to Isaac a letter sent to her by her brother Jonas:

'My dear Sister, ... If I was in your place I should use great caution ... it is your duty to be guided a little by your family ... In the higher families it is a (custom) for Settlement to be made upon the female before marrying... if you take such a risky step without a proper settlement you will forfeit all claim to reasonable precaution... for you to place yourself in the hand of Mr Holden without a proper provision would be madness'.

Isaac's initial response was conditional:

> *'I approve of your brothers requiring it for your benefit in case of any fortuitous event, which may occur in future life. I would only remark that must be made on the principle that you are all my own that all you own should become mine in reality, though placed justly beyond my control during your life'.*

However his next letter reveals that his search for a 'prudent wife' extended beyond his courtship of Sarah:

> *When I first wrote to you I had made up my mind to get married. I considered it necessary for my well being as well as my domestic comfort and to get a good wife as soon as possible. In looking about me I had cast my eye upon two amiable ladies, yourself the first ... Had I met with the misfortune of your refusal it was my intention to make an offer of immediate marriage to a lady who I had every reason to be assured would accept my offer at once. This I learned without giving the least idea of my thinking of her... What should be my feelings when it is proposed to defer all decision till another Spring?*

Turning to the terms of the marriage settlement, Isaac reflected the patriarchal attitudes of the period:

> *Prudence dictates the propriety of a provision for the comfort and security of the "weaker vessel" should misfortune or dire widowhood avail ... I am pleased by your reference to my family ... You know their previous mother watched over them with a pious solicitude, was strict in her discipline and did not spoil them in their infancy nor afterwards by unkind indulgence.*

This makes them much more agreeable than if they had been pampered by a mother whom they remember with affection.

He also began to prepare Sarah for his expectations of the marriage bed, writing:

'The matter of marriage and the conjugal relation has a principle deeply founded in the secret places of our nature and therefore it excites the most intense feeling. We are therefore justified in allowing our feelings to take strong hold in the affair'.

And in another letter, written in December:

'Well we must be patient till the spring (when) We shall no longer reciprocate thought and feeling through the pen but through the converse kindness and pure pleasure of married life … the highest conduction of earthly bliss and the desire of which he has deeply implanted in our natures'.

Surprisingly frank in revealing her ignorance of sexual matters in her next letter Sarah had again been troubled by friends giving more details of Isaac's earlier relationships:

'I am looking forward with pleasure when a kind providence will permit you to complete my earthly bliss and advance my heavenly joy, but not without trembling feelings arising from the importance and responsibility connected with such enjoyment. If our union is to take place any where near to the time you refer to, will it not be well for us to lie saying something of its proceedings and what will be required.

> *Since I wrote to you last I have met with persons giving me information of you ... It was told you had given an offer to Mrs Craven and Miss Rouse and some others, but the greatest stress they laid on these two. ...They wished to acquaint Miss Sugden that Mr Holden had lost all his property in Bradford.*

> *Had you not told me that you had never at any time offered yourself but to two persons, & I have no doubt that your memory will remind you who they are, I might have passed it by as a fact without thinking more of it. I think I should not have given it you at present, but thinking an explanation from you will prepare me if I am similarly appraised to either to confront or be silent. I have a secret feeling that the parties do not have the most friendly feelings towards you'.*

He blamed his enemies for spreading malicious rumours:

> *The old enemy is still at work but happily without success in his object... I confess having entertained some thoughts of both the parties named, chiefly in consequence of the strong recommendations of friends.*

> *Miss R I had never seen and know her only from report. I was induced to write to her from the very strong and pressing recommendations of a near relation of hers who assured me of success.... Afterwards when I learned her age I thought she acted very wisely. So far what you heard was true but nothing more. As to making offers to Mrs C and several others – it is all false. One female who knew my mother's views by being much at our house named the thing to Mrs C in a way I disapproved of and so as*

> *perhaps to produce an impression on Mrs C's mind that an offer was made, but though I was told Mrs C did not positively object, I never saw her more though otherwise I should certainly have done so even from old friendship with her and her late husband*
>
> *In referring back to circumstances, which transpired in the first 12 or 15 months after my late dear wife's death, a strange feeling comes over me. My mind was much weakened by distracting and solitary grief which made me lack for counsel and comfort in a way I was unaccustomed to, and which made me feel the truth of the proverb gain and again – "A prudent wife is from the Lord." I shall feel happy when the sanction of providence stamps my choice by the fact of our union and gives me another prudent wife.*

Sarah, who knew 'Mrs C', was not entirely happy with this explanation:

> *… I certainly could not have brought my mind to think that your mind would ever think of making Mrs C your Amie. The grief and sorrow, which you might be overwhelmed with in your position at the time I think I can make allowance for.*

The matter is never referred to again in their correspondence. Their attention now returned to the terms of the marriage settlement. Isaac sought to secure the interests of his children:

'23 February 1850 ... I have today received a letter from Mr Jonas with a copy of the Marriage Settlement, which is quite satisfactory to me.

I wish my present children to know that by your marriage with me you adopt them to all intents and purposes as your children and that they may therefore confidently and affectionately rely upon you as their Mother... and that any property you may have shall be equally divided between them and your own children.

Before our marriage I intend to speak openly to my children on the subject ... I shall read it to them - "In becoming a mother to your family.... All that I have shall be theirs in the same share as my own children and I hope they will be good obedient and affectionate to me as their mother. I posses property at my disposal and immediately after my marriage I shall make a Will to that above effect"...If you can fully and cordially write the above it will serve to me the same purpose as if it were placed in the Marriage Settlement'.

Sarah turned to her brothers for advice before replying:

'I told Bros your opinion in reference to the settlement before anything was done, but they appeared to think that such a thing should not at all be mentioned to the children.

The advice on one side and your request on the other what am I to do? Will it not be better to have a little personal consultation and explanation, and if you decidedly think it the best, it can be done... My sentiments are perfectly the same as when I gave you, for the family to be one without any distinction'.

He remained insistent that Sarah makes a Will:

'I cannot bear the idea of the Husband and wife having two interests. Although I cordially consent to a marriage settlement to secure your portion during life time yet I must insist upon the fusion of our interests into one by your making a Will as soon as may be after the marriage bequeathing to me and to our family all your disposable fortune after your death. I should reserve to you the power of cutting off any of my children who might not manifest the duty and affection of children to a mother, as I should do myself it they proved themselves unworthy'.

Sarah, who knew her own mind, stood her ground:

'When Bros prepared what they thought ought to be done in the Settlement I hesitated to the proposal thinking it might not meet your views but when they proposed it being at my own disposal I felt relieved and agreed to it, concluding then that it would be betwixed you and me. I do assure you that you my be easy on that… I have no doubt that we shall make it agreeable betwixed ourselves'.

Sarah and Isaac were married in April 1850. Mr Edward Townsend of Cullingworth acted as groomsman.

5. New Beginnings.

Le Grand Barrage

Returning to France in February 1849 Isaac rented a former wool combing mill, 'Le Grand Barrage', at St Denis to the north of Paris. The location was chosen partly because there was already a textile industry in the town and also because of its proximity to Paris, where legal matters relating to patents could be resolved. Tavernier, Lister's agent, had an office in Paris and Isaac later claimed that St Denis was chosen for his benefit.

During this first year a version of the 'working comb' was used in trials at Le Grand Barrage together with locally procured old carding engines. Isaac employed mechanics from England to assist in installing the machines and, as he was to do later in his other factories, employed his fellow countrymen as supervisors. Lister, who was having considerable difficulties in getting the Square Motion to work efficiently in England, continued to press Isaac to use the Nip machine and delayed sending Square Motions out to France. Once they arrived Isaac persisted over long hours and months with the development of the Square Motion despite Lister's continuing reservations about the considerable costs of Isaac's experimentation: 'Such a large sum expended in making a beginning is to me incomprehensible.'

By the end of the first year of trading Le Grand Barrage had begun to be productive but it was not until the summer of 1850 that the corner was turned and it began to return a profit. His two nephews, Isaac Holden Crothers and Jonathan Holden, who were to play significant roles in the growing concern, joined the business that year.

The Education of Boys and Girls

His family moved to live with Isaac in a house adjoining the factory. The children appear to have been out of school for much of the year. His ward, Eliza Townsend, for whom there was a trust fund, remained at school in England. Angus and Edward were sent to a boarding school in the Rue de Chevreuse in Paris for a few months in 1850 and to a school in Edinburgh the following year. Edward then moved to the Sion House Academy in Jersey and to the Wesleyan School at Soham outside Cambridge the next year. The head teacher of Sion School in October 1852 wrote on Edward's report card, 'we find him lamentably backward in Arithmetic. He must have been very badly taught…. We perceive many ways in which he needs polishing.'

In contrast with his attitude to the education of boys Isaac informed Sarah he had engaged a governess for the girls:

> *I am going to engage the sister of Mr Field, our second preacher, as governess for my two daughters. I don't wish my daughters to go from home to school, as there are often habits there, which estrange them from their parents and make them disagreeable.*

Under pressure from Sarah he sent Mary and Margaret to school in England the following year. Sarah had found a suitable school, the Moravian School for Young Ladies at Gomersal, the fees being 24 guineas plus two and a half guineas for washing. The prospectus noted that 'Each pupil has a separate bed'; pupils were required to bring with them, bed linen, towels, a silver teapot and desert spoons. Mary wrote a plaintive letter in her first term asking Sarah if she had arranged how the girls would get to France for the summer holidays.

The girls spent two years at Gomersal. The older of the two sisters, Mary, now turned 17, wanted a greater degree of independence than Gomersal offered. She wrote to her father listing her objections to staying on there and stating her preference to move to a 'finishing school' as a 'kind of parlour border', which would 'combine more of the social feeling of home with school life.' She wanted to be able 'to go out as I liked' and 'I should not wish to go to bed before 10 o'clock and I would like to have my supper in my own room.' When Edward failed to come to the school to collect them at the end of term - he was shopping in Harrogate – the head teacher would not let them make their own way to an aunt in Dockroyd because they were not chaperoned. Mary wrote complaining to her father, 'It is very thoughtless of him. All the ladies went home yesterday and Margaret and I are the only two left.'

Transfer to the Priory School in Pontefract in the autumn term of 1855 was again organised by Sarah who knew the two 'Misses Watts' who ran it. The curriculum included arithmetic, French, German and Italian, music, ornamental needlework and lessons in wax flowers, drawing, and the use of globes, calisthentetics and dancing. Mary was accepted as a 'parlour border'. After the first year they lifted their restrictions on letter writing for Mary so that they would no longer read her letters before they were sent. Their father was an irregular correspondent and Maggie once wrote complaining to Sarah that she had not written for nine weeks. Indeed in 1857 Mary was at school for a whole half year without seeing her father and both girls spent the Christmas of 1856 with the Misses Watts.

Correspondence between Isaac and the Miss Watts was quite informal and they were invited to visit St Denis. However in April 1857 he took them to task for allowing the girls to stay an extra day with Miss Pickles and Eliza Townsend instead of returning to school after the Easter holiday. The Miss Watts responded agreeing 'another time we shall be more stringent.'

Mary left school at the age of 18 in the summer of 1857. Margaret stayed for a while longer before she was sent to Laleham Lodge in Clapham, a 'progressive school for young ladies' run by Mrs and Miss Pipe; the fees were £100 per year and Maggie stayed there until 1860. Isaac wrote to Maggie on 10th June 1858, 'Your future happiness depends much on a well cultivated mind and still more on possessing those heavenly graces which a Christian faith only can beget in your spirit'. She wrote to her father, 'I should like you to see us at our gymnastics, performing all sorts of things with our arms and legs. We wear costumes in which we can move about without much inconvenience.'

Mary had an unsought for suitor that October and wrote to her father asking his advice on what she should do: 'he is a young man I could not love…Therefore I want to know what you think I should say to him.'

A Manly Husband

In the spring of 1850 Sarah first travelled to France and was feted at Le Grand Barrage by 'the whole of the workpeople entering the gates in procession with a band of music and the firing of cannon.' On her arrival she bemoaned finding that 'Mr Holden has left the management of the house entirely to servants and whatever has been wanted has not been refused so that the expense has been great. I see no advantage yet in their manner and far less comfort.'

She wrote instructing Isaac to make changes in the management of the household before her return. His male pride piqued, he rebuked her for saying "I shall feel on my return much grieved if it is not done":

> *I cannot think you mean you will be grieved at me as it cannot in that case be an expression for a good wife to address her Husband. It is the way I should speak to my servant with whom I intended to be rough and severe... You know my principle is that between Husband and Wife the language and manner dictated by a gentle and tender affection is always the best; and especially submission by a wife to a Husband's judgment combined with affectionate counsel is most influential with a manly Husband.*

Sarah disliked living in France; although she spent several months there each year she never learned to speak French fluently. Isaac spoke French fluently; he read Mme Lesbazeille-Souvestre's translation of Jayne Eyre in French when it was first published in France in 1854. Over the next 8 years Sarah continually tried to persuade Isaac to move back to England. When she first visited Paris in 1850 she wrote disapprovingly to her brother:

> *Mr Holden shewed (sic) me some parts of Paris, in order to give me some idea how the Sabbath was spent, but I do assure you it gave me no pleasure, but great pain.*

The couple even spent their first Christmas as a married couple apart; in her absence the gregarious Isaac had treated the workforce of 350 to a New Year dinner at a restaurant in the town.

Of a melancholic disposition Sarah shunned company outside her immediate family back home at Oakworth to which she regularly retreated for months on end. Isaac wrote urging her to:

> *Be cheerful and gay and throw yourself without fear into all the cheerful innocent hilarity of good society, chase away gloom as a vitiating and dangerous thing. Don't be afraid of committing sin by being cheerful and even playful.*

But the marriage had got off to a poor start and he was disturbed by her continuing absences. He wrote challenging her on July 10th 1851, 'You seem to be so much happier with your brothers and among your old friends than with me... I certainly should not wish you to come here and be unhappy; and with your present views and feelings it seems to me you cannot be happy to return.' The letter goes on, 'the tone of all your letters and especially your last – That married life should be one of "sorrow" - I do not understand. The expression of such a feeling gives me intense pain.'

Although their union seems not to have been "the highest conduction of earthly bliss and the desire" Isaac had hoped for, the couple shared a missionary zeal which nevertheless bound them together spiritually if not physically. Sarah continued to regard Catholic France with deep suspicion. Isaac built a small Wesleyan chapel at St Denis, which her brother noted approvingly would make her 'better satisfied with France.' The family regularly worshipped at the Wesleyan meeting room at the rue de l'Oratoire in Paris and he became a member of its Finance Committee, attending the French

Wesleyan Conference on their behalf in 1853. Sarah gave a donation to the chapel on the rue de l'Ortaire. The Minister, somewhat mischievously, thanked her for her financial support 'in the work of Christ in this gay, wicked city'.

Almost inevitable destruction

Sarah remained in close contact with her brothers whilst in France. Their relationship with her nephew, William Craven, gives another insight into how the Sugden's viewed the social conventions of Victorian marriage. Her nephew, William, had fallen in love with and wanted to marry one of the Sugden's mill workers, Martha Feather. The Sugden brothers strongly disapproved, warning William failing to choose someone of his own rank would lead to his 'almost inevitable destruction'. Bored with their social conventions William stood his ground writing in July 1853 to tell them that, 'as to choosing one of my own ranks, there are but a few of the young ladies of the present day that bring much profit with them, for such is the society now that most of them must either have an establishment quite equal to the home they have left or it will not do'. In Pygmalion style he advised his uncles that Martha would 'leave their employ on August 3rd. . I shall then put her under a course of improvement and then send her away to someone at a distance for a time, and if we are both spared, ultimately marry her.'

Sarah wrote to William in October castigating him for the course he had taken, 'my feelings for you ensure against all judgement of the mind induces me to try another time. … You are on the direct road to ruining both your soul and body and before you are aware you will have brought yourself and family to poverty.' In August 1855 William wrote to his aunt asking if he could bring his wife to see her in France but she turned down his request. However her attitude appears to have softened over time and on December 21st 1857 he wrote thanking her for a gift she had sent him, 'I am not teetotal, but on that hand am very much improved'. By this time William's father, John Craven, was in Paris working with Isaac.

Don't be jealous

The majority of the mechanics and supervisors who came to St Denis from Bradford and Scotland were fellow Nonconformists. Whilst they were not compelled to attend chapel it is clear that they were prudent to do so. In a speech to the workers at the annual Christmas dinner Isaac said:

> *Let me recommend religion - don't be jealous, I will regard you without prejudice if possible if you are not religious – but I would choose a religious man and love him more who would not, if rightly informed.*

There are echoes in this speech of Isaac's brother in law, Jonas Sugden, who put up posters in his own factory exhorting his workers to attend worship. The pious Jonas would not employ gamblers or drinkers, and ordered those who were cohabiting to marry or be dismissed.

Tensions with Lister's agent Tavernier, who had been successful in bringing in commissioned work largely from the Baron de Fourment, began to emerge. The relationship was made more difficult by Tavernier's relationship with Donnisthorpe, who was to become his brother-in-law, and whom Isaac now suspected of planning to set up a rival firm in France. Isaac made a note of Tavernier's faults in preparation for a meeting with Lister:

> *'Altogether Tavernier has shown too much apathy – sitting at home and depending on the Baron instead of*

expanding his commissions with other Houses... (he has also) allowed himself to be hoaxed into an order double (sic) of Donnisthorpe'.

Coup d'état

On December 2nd 1851 Louis Napoleon staged his *coup d'état* and on 4th the "massacre of the boulevards" took place in Paris. Three days later Isaac wrote reassuring Sarah:

'We are now all quiet here and at Paris. Why we have all been quiet here and worked as usual, but in Paris there has been some uneasiness and some bloodshed and destruction of property... some 300 have been killed. There is no doubt that order will be strictly maintained... Our men came to say that there would be no attempt to disturb us but if there was they would hazard their lives to defend us'.

As a businessman Isaac craved order and consistently put this ahead of his liberal sympathies when judging Louis Napoleon. He wrote to Sarah on the day of the plebiscite (December 21st), paving the way for Napoleon's Second Empire, saying he had been told by one of Napoleon's most influential advisers that, 'Napoleon desires much to ameliorate the conditions of the lower classes of the country, to improve its institutions, that he is a gifted and well informed man and possesses the power by his *name* and skill to establish and preserve the most perfect order in the country.' Adding, 'Have Brothers seen Napoleon's manifesto on the observance of the Sabbath? He speaks strongly of the observance of the Sabbath.'

After the plebiscite a new authoritarian constitution was introduced by Napoleon. More than 26,000 arrests were made including the Deputies of the late Chamber - not quite the little "uneasiness" Isaac had described to Sarah. Strict censorship was introduced, which may well account for some of Isaac's caution in offering any criticism of Louis Napoleon in his correspondence. The new Chamber was filled with successful businessmen, which may offer another explanation for Isaac's apparent acquiescence with the new regime.

Bones of Contention

By the summer of 1852 Lister had become uneasy about the unstable political position in France that was being reported very negatively in the British press. [The French Constitution prohibited the re-election of the President for a second term and this was the cause of political turmoil that summer.] In panic Lister wrote urging Isaac to:

> *'Sell up every shillings worth of stock that you have. I want everything turned into money except of course the machinery... not to run any risk of what may take place ... as to who is to be President or King'.*

Lister now threatened Isaac with the dissolution of the partnership, describing his conduct in withholding remittances back to England as "shameful". He wrote to him in July asserting that Isaac's figures, which suggested a cash balance of £18,000, were incorrect, 'Tavernier writes the stock will not pay the debts. Who am I too believe?' Lister's partner at Manningham, Mr. Ambler, was urgently dispatched to France to check the books, but found them to be in order.

There were still two major bones of contention between the partners. Firstly, their longstanding disagreement over which machine to adopt, the Nip or the Square Motion comb, and secondly, Tavernier's role in the enterprise exacerbated by Lister having mooted offering him a partnership. On December 25th 1851 Isaac wrote a letter, which was to become critically important in their later dispute about the origins of the Square Motion comb. In this letter Isaac strongly resisted giving a partnership to Tavernier and laid claim to developing the Square Motion comb, 'After you had, at least for the time, laid it aside as useless for fine wool, I took it out of the corner, rubbed the dust of it, and have worked it out to its present very efficient practical superiority.' Notwithstanding Isaac's advice, Lister signed a form of agreement with Tavernier in January 1852 giving him the option of becoming a partner instead of being on commission. Lister later claimed never to have read the document before signing it until Tavernier gave notice of choosing to exercise the option the following year.

The partners now began to look for new premises for the business to expand. A factory site at Croix, on the outskirts of Roubaix in the Nord region, was selected and Isaac's other nephew, Isaac Holden Crothers put in charge. Construction of a new factory was also started in Rheims with his nephew, Jonathan Holden, in charge. Production at both the new factories started in 1853.

The Master Strategist

Samuel Lister, as committed to the 'Nip' as Isaac Holden was to the Square Motion, was prepared to go to considerable lengths to protect his patent. Schlumberger, who owned the patent to Heilmann's version of the 'nip', saw Lister's machine as an infringement. He took Lister to court in France in 1852 and won his claim. In a blocking move Lister, forever the master strategist, promptly paid £30,000 for the rights to sell Heilmann's comb in England, stopped its production there, and promoted his own comb as a virtual monopoly. He also later moved to purchase all of Schlumberger's French wool combing patents in 1856 but found he had been duped by Tavernier, who had already allegedly acquired the right to make charges on their use in partnership with Donnisthorpe thus confirming Isaac's earlier suspicions about Donnisthorpe's French aspirations. This time Isaac came to the rescue and astutely negotiated with Donnisthorpe in June 1857 to pay £35,000 for half of Schlumberger's patents to be transferred to Lister Holden, thus giving them a virtual monopoly in France.

Like a strawberry in the mouth of an elephant

In the second half of 1853 Lister ran into cash flow problems with his Bradford businesses and began to panic about the likelihood of war in Crimea:

> *'There are some reports flying around about the Russians entering Turkey and that war is certain… You should lose no time in securing a mortgage if you can on good terms; if there should be a war it would be impossible to obtain money and we might all be on our beam-ends'.*

Throughout the autumn Lister continued to urge the mortgaging of the mills. He wrote to Isaac on New Years Eve:

> *'What annoys and vexes me is that I made a special journey to France because Tavernier wrote to me to say that the mortgage money when received would be "like a strawberry in the mouth of an elephant"'.*

The following summer Lister's business in England again experienced severe cash flow problems. He wrote to Isaac admonishing him for failing to remit more money back to England. 'I have

£70,000 in the French concern and not been able to get a shilling is a rascally shame and I consider you the cause of it.'

On August 2nd Isaac wrote to Sarah saying, 'Mr Lister is going to be married to a very wealthy lady of high family. If so, it may get him out of his troubles for a time.' Triggered by this news, Isaac's thoughts now turned to his own Marriage Settlement and he wrote to Sarah suggesting that she ask her brothers to pay her the interest on her capital from the time of their marriage as, 'It is worth little to Brothers and it is worth 5 per cent at least to us.' He also wrote to Jonas, 'While we were in a little hazard owing to Mr Lister's indiscreet outlay of capital even with a good business I did not care about drawing it, but now that I think all danger has ceased it will be well to draw it.' Jonas wrote back the following day agreeing to pay the interest on the marriage settlement. Isaac's true motive for writing to Jonas emerged in his next letter to Sarah written on September 6th, 'I am not a little harassed with some nasty affairs in business, the result of Tavernier's conduct … I hope we shall soon be able to pay him off whatever he might do to injure us.'

By Superior Orders

The fear that Tavernier might sue for breach of contract over Lister's agreement giving him the option of becoming a partner dominated the correspondence between the two principal partners over the next few months. Isaac made a note in his Notebook, 'Tavernier threatens to commence action if we don't settle. Mr L seems disposed to accept him. I will not on any conditions.'

Angus Holden, who was overseeing the factory at St Denis in Isaac's absence, wrote providing an amusing insight onto Tavernier's character:

> 'Tavernier like a little tom fool comes bobbing in every morning swishing his wig and spitting most furiously, asking me convivially if Mr Holden has not returned. This morning he asked, from my replying in the negative, he said that you must have been seized with the cholera... he must be beginning to think himself a powerful fellow... Do father get rid of him'.

Isaac did all he could to drive Tavernier out of the business altogether by withdrawing his cooperation. Tavernier wrote an outraged letter of protest to Lister:

> 'Dear Sir, by superior orders of Mr Holden, I must not send you any money or discount any more bills accepted by you.
>
> By superior orders, I am no more to have anything to do with the customers in Rheims or Croix.
>
> By superior orders, all the bills or remittances must be sent direct to Mr Holden at St Denis.
>
> By superior orders, all I have to do is get my commissions: Amen!
>
> P.S. We have at our banks £6,000. What is due I do not know and cannot know, Amen!'

A vituperative letter from Lister accused Isaac of being 'hypocritical' in his dealings with Tavernier, and in not consenting to refund a proportion of the capital, 'Your conduct is abominable ... I will put an end to the partnership'. Isaac secured a mortgage of £6,000 against the Croix property. He also turned to Jonas Sugden offering to secure the Rheims property against a loan if he could get his brothers to agree, but they declined to do so unless Lister was part of the agreement. Jonas was sympathetic to Isaac and wrote to him on Boxing Day advising him that he should stick to his guns and call Lister's bluff, 'if he will have Tavernier he must part with you'.

Tavernier was planning to set up a rival business with Donnisthorpe and, at the same time, he brought a legal action against Isaac staking his claim to be a partner of Lister & Holden and claiming a share of the profits. Rather than risk seeing him decamp to a rival concern, Lister urged Isaac to reach an out of court settlement. He was also intent on preventing Donnisthorpe introducing the rival Noble wool-combing machine, of which Donnisthorpe owned the patent, into France. He told Isaac that, if he could not conclude a deal to buy the Noble patent from Donnisthorpe (and thus preserve his monopoly in France), he would rather sell his shares in Lister & Holden than 'to have opposition, especially from a formidable machine like Noble'.

The Collett Affair: the Baron has been so shifty

In the meantime Tavernier had been putting it about that Holden & Lister was retaining the waste from their customers' wool and in May 1855 Isaac had a summons served against him in relation to the matter by one of his customers, Collett. The reputational damage in losing such a case as this, the *Collett affair*, would have been enough to ruin not only the partner's business as commission combers in France, but could also have been very injurious to Lister's interests in Bradford where the case was being followed closely.

As part of a strategy to force Isaac to sell his share of the business, Donnisthorpe and Tavernier were now proposing to give evidence in support of Collett alleging that they had seen large amounts of waste wool at the warehouse in St Denis belonging to Holden & Lister's customers. Tavernier had even employed an agent, Simpson, who had been dismissed by Lister & Holden, to find out if it was the practice in Bradford to retain their customers' waste and to find out if Isaac had left debts behind when Pit Lane failed.

Tavernier also threatened to use letters in which Lister had made allegations about Isaac's mismanagement of the firm in the Collett case. Lister promptly wrote a statement saying that he had since learnt the allegations he had made about Isaac's mismanagement were false. He also applied pressure on Tavernier and Donnisthorpe to withdraw this evidence and wrote advising Isaac, 'It is in both Donnisthorpe and Tavernier's interest to help you if you do not provoke them.' An eyewitness at the Collett tribunal hearing vividly described:

> *'The scene of that day at the Palais de Justice is ineffaceably fixed on my mental retina and in all the picture there is non such relief and contrast as between your placidity and self-possession as his (Tavernier's) unrest and Satanic contortions. Shakespeare says not a fraction more than the truth in the well repeated line'.*

The court having found in Isaac's favour in the Collett case in August, he wrote to Lister saying, 'I know how to appreciate Tavernier's help and honesty. I never wanted him to help me. As to Mr Donnisthorpe if I did not believe that he has been deceived by the rogues he has dealt with I should never speak to him more.' The case dragged on in the courts of appeal but was finally settled in Isaac's favour at the end of December with costs awarded to Isaac.

A blush of shame

The anxiety created by the Collett affair so stirred Sarah that she went to Lister's home in October and challenged him about his role in it. Clearly irked, his response was to write a frank and revealing letter to Isaac drawing to his attention to:

> *'A few of the leading facts which I hope you will read to your wife as I told her I would do nothing that the whole world should not know, and I am sure she must feel a blush of shame when she sees how I have been treated by you who owe everything to me…*
>
> *Mr Donnisthorpe declared that you had insulted him… and he would have his revenge as he would go into court and say that he had seen at St Denis, … as much wool in your warehouse taken from the customers as would hang half a dozen men in England and … finding that nothing would satisfy him of your good faith but a document that when the Collett affair was over that the concern would be sold… I gave him a Memorandum to that affect. I have no doubt that it was that document that saved you from being condemned – upon the strength of it he bought off Collett and he compelled Tavernier and other witnesses to say that they thought you had taken the wool without intending to rob'.*

Rumours circulated that Isaac had bought Collett off and Isaac subsequently made an entry in his Notebook on November 17th in preparation for the final Collett hearing, 'Should show letters… and also Mr Lister's letter in which he speaks of buying off Donnisthorpe'. However he did not do so.

Isaac had a retrospective discussion with Tavernier about the Collett affair in 1857:

> *'Tavernier says Lister's letter proves that he took common cause against me at the time through the influence of*

Donnisthorpe. Collett affair was brought in to force me to sell my part and the noise of the sale and the formation of the company was to convey the impression that I sought to escape from the condemnation aimed at in the lawsuit. Hence my letter begging Lister not to sell, nor to mix himself in any way in the noise of it'.

Had Isaac been hoarding his customers waste wool?

J. M. Trickett, a researcher who carried out a 'Technological Appraisal of the Isaac Holden Papers', found entries in Isaac's Notebooks in 1853 that refer to the disposal of waste wool, which had apparently been re-combed and sold as 'tops'. Isaac had been instructed by Lister in 1853 to 'comb and sell your waste.' However Isaac had issued instructions at that time to be careful to keep waste separate and ensure that the conditions upon which combing was undertaken was well understood by the customer. Trickett also found in his 1854 Notebooks that he had quantified the benefits of adjusting settings so as to decrease the proportion of 'robbings' (a technical term but an unfortunate one) on the increased quantities of 'top' and 'noil' produced. A detailed costing showed that what Lister & Holden lost to the customer through this adjustment was to some extent offset by the saving in the cost of reworking the 'robbings'. However it may also have led to the enlarged quantity of surplus wool waste which Tavernier and Donnisthorpe claimed to have seen at the St Dennis factory.

Lister's claim that, after he had applied pressure, Donnisthorpe had 'bought off Collett' and 'compelled Tavernier and other witnesses' to say that Isaac had 'taken the wool without intending to rob' would be, if true, very damaging to Isaac's reputation. However the rapid growth of the business over the next five years seems to suggest that their customers accepted the court decision and did not move their commission-combing elsewhere.

6. Cité Anglaise

The Lister Holden factory at Croix, the heart of the French textile industry, quickly became the town's largest employer. Thirty-eight of his fellow countrymen were brought in when the factory started to act as managers, supervisors and skilled mechanics. Within a few years he had created a miniature "cité anglaise" with new housing for his English and Scottish workers.

Expenditure on the needs of the local workforce tended to reflect Isaac's own preoccupations with religion and education. A chapel with a schoolroom was built at Croix in 1861, to be looked after by the Minister, Charles Faulkner, who had started out as a workman and lay preacher at St Denis. Isaac preached at the chapel once a month. A day school was also built the same year and the daughter of the Wesleyan preacher put in charge. Eventually a mechanics' institute was added and a small proportion of the company's profits were used to finance a bandstand, retirement home and town cemetery with an area for the incomers. Amongst those buried in the Croix cemetery are Isaac's sister, Agnes, and her husband his manager, Isaac Holden Crothers, after whom a street was named and remains to this day, together with Crothers second wife, Mary Faulkner, and other members of the Faulkner, Metcalfe, Gemmel, Overall and Lewthwait families. The company also paid for the local fire brigade, fire being an ever-present hazard in a wool factory, and a railway junction so that goods could get in and out.

Likewise at Reims, Lister & Holden built new housing for its French and English workers who lived in 'La Colonie Anglaise'. A communal washhouse, lecture hall, games and recreation room, school, and Wesleyan chapel were also built near the factory.

Such apparent philanthropy in meeting the needs of the workforce was not uncommon amongst manufacturers in this period. For example W.E. Forster and his partner William Fison had built a factory school and library at their manufacturing village at Burley in Wharfedale and Titus Salt went further with his elaborate model village in Saltaire, Bradford.

Isaac's philanthropy was partly informed by a need to placate the local authorities for the pollution caused by his factories. In June 1856 Jonathan Holden wrote to Isaac telling him:

> *'The authorities of Reims are making much ado about our suds standing around Gosset's property from which arises a strange stench especially along in front of the caserne (soldiers billet), which makes them afraid it will be injurious to the health of the soldiers and public generally. So last Friday we were invited to appear before the Mayor and his satellites …they had come to the conclusion our suds had become a nuisance by the many complaints that had been sent to them… It is only as I have been expecting for some time, for there is really a strong smell that can be felt at a distance from the factory'.*

Not only was wool combing polluting it was potentially lethal. There was a risk of anthrax, known as the "woolsorters' disease" or pointedly in France as "la maladie de Bradford" because of the clusters of reports of the disease in the area which were highlighted in press reports in the 1870s. The "Bradford Rules" requiring better ventilation and cleansing in the rooms in which wool was sorted were created in an effort to prevent the spread of the disease. The general working conditions in the woolcombing factories were uncomfortable and hazardous with the temperature in the combing rooms at times being unbearable. In 1861 a boiler burst at Reims leaving six men dead and four injured, the same year William Outhwaite was taken round the shaft at Croix and killed instantly. Isaac himself had his own hand squeezed in a machine in 1860 from which he made a painfully slow recovery. Jonas Holmes who worked as a head 'fireman' or stoker at the Holden's Alston Works in Bradford died as the result of an industrial accident there when one of the boilers exploded in 1871. He lingered painfully for about three months and then died of his injuries leaving his wife with three small boys.

The Pledge.

Two rules were paramount in Isaac's mills, No Smoking and No Drinking. Isaac was an inveterate cigar smoker - preferring Maduro to Colorado cigars - but presumably followed his own factory rules on site. He had signed 'The Pledge' against strong drink in 1830 but drank wine in France, partly because of the lack of ready access to fresh water supplies. When he moved back to England in the early 1860s he bought in large quantities of fine wines. In 1871 he held £1,600 shares in a champagne company, but the investment was later written off in his accounts as 'moonshine!' He would also later arrange for shipments of fine wine to England for his sons and daughters. However he remained a strong advocate against any form of drunkenness amongst his employees. There are many examples in his papers of his counselling those of his employees who drank heavily, including one Thomas Froy who on 22nd June 1855 signed a pledge:

> 'I hereby engage to drink no brandy, wine, beer of fermented liquors of any kind during the next 12 months. If I should break this engagement I herby also engage to forfeit to Mr Holden any money I may leave on his hands as my saving. X. His Mark'

Honeyman and Goodman have calculated that under the direct management of Isaac's nephew, Isaac Crothers, production at the factory at Croix grew at an astonishing average annual rate of 29 per cent between 1854 and 1861. Production at Reims under the direction of Jonathan Holden grew more slowly but still averaged an impressive annual rate of 14.3 per cent over the same period. With a quarter of the market share of all combed wool in France, profits at the Croix and Reims were to reach £10,000 per month in the 1860s and 1870s (equivalent to £771,000 in today's terms using the RPI calculator at www.measuringworth.com). Rivalry between the two nephews was a key feature of the developing business, coming to a head in the 1860s. As early as January 1856 Jonathan felt he was being unfairly treated when Isaac refused him a pay rise.

Isaac's sons were both involved in the business in the second half of the 1850s; Angus deputising for Isaac at St Denis and Edward spending time at Reims. Isaac lived quite modestly in the house at St Denis and Angus was always asking him to "box it up a bit". He and Mary, who moved to St Denis after leaving school, took this in hand and refurbished the house in the spring of 1858 when Angus wrote telling him, 'so now we are comfortable and decent'. Isaac complained to Sarah, 'In some things they have gone further than I would and in others I would have bought something finer.'

A cloak fit for the Emperor

Under the authoritarian Empire of Louis Napoleon, the Commissaries appointed by him to major cities played a key role in exercising political surveillance and keeping order. At the end of 1856 when there was a severe downturn in trade in Reims and high levels of unemployment, the Commisaire played a special visit to Jonathan Holden at the factory and requested 'a private conversation' with him, demanding to know:

> 'If I knew that we had any men that conversed or interfered in politics in any way, or complained of dear living, or that in any way were disposed to blame the government for either want of work or bread. I replied that I had never heard of any murmurs hostile to the existing government ... and added our hands thus far had had no occasion to complain, as they had always been fully employed and well paid'.

Jonathan was instructed by the Commisaire to inform him if there were to be any reduction in the workforce, and to 'enquire particularly of your overlookers of the conduct of their hands, if they are difficult to manage or if there is any instigator to anything.' Jonathan saw the Commisaire's instructions as 'indications of and natural to a despotic government, yea and even necessary to its existence'.

Isaac took a more moderate approach to the regime, describing the opening of the Paris Exhibition a few months earlier he told Sarah, 'the Emperor spoke like a man having authority and able to use it.' He went on to boast how at the opening, 'I happened by the greatest chance to wear a coat on the occasion made for the Emperor'. His tailor had offered him one of two coats he had made for the Emperor, who was similarly small in stature, and so he had bought it. Mary seems to have been as impressed by the Emperor as her father. 'I must tell you we had a beautiful view of the Emperor and Empress, and for the first time the Imperial Prince', she wrote to her sister on February 19th 1858.

Boxers at Law

In the summer of 1856 Lister learnt that Donnisthorpe, Crofts and Tavernier had taken a mill near Paris and were planning to use a modified Noble comb. His response was typically strategic, moving ahead with plans to purchase rival patents in order to squeeze out any opposition. It is noticeable that his letters to Isaac at this time were written in a neater hand, more familiar in tone and less florid than when he was annoyed with or abusing him. This time Lister's ire was saved for Donnisthorpe who he felt had betrayed his trust by sharing with Tavernier correspondence that indicated he was willing to pay him the disputed commission.

In the second half of 1857, there was a severe economic and banking crisis. Several provincial banks collapsed in northern England and Lister's business interests in Halifax, where the Western Bank collapsed, were very badly affected. In November, Brown, Lister's partner in his Halifax concern, urged Isaac to raise as much cash as he could to help them. In December, James Sugden wrote to Isaac from Bradford warning, 'I think it would be well for you to be guarded for it appears that Lister is so engulfed in difficulties over such a vortex that if you are not very careful you will be drawn into it.' Angus also wrote urging, 'If he is not wishful to sell, wait until all gets in the hands of his creditors.'

The French economy also experienced a severe economic downturn. Credit lines were temporarily cut off and in Reims Jonathan had to beg the bank for money to pay the wages.

Once again the partners had opposing interests. Lister urgently needed cash but wanted to retain his share of the business, whilst Isaac had begun to formulate a plan to set his two sons up in business as worsted spinners in Bradford and wanted to accumulate funds in order to do so. The profits generated had enabled Isaac to accumulate capital. Lister wrote to Isaac on January 1st 1858 telling him he needed to raise £33,000 to pay a bank mortgage that was being called in and offered to have a new deed of partnership drafted, but not to reduce his share in the business. He wrote to him again a fortnight later chiding him for being slow in responding, 'Give us all you can', he begged. Isaac agreed to forward more cash 'to avoid the disgrace of Brown's stoppage.' By the end of January Isaac had remitted a total of £30,000 (equivalent to over £2.6 million in today's terms) over the previous three months.

Lister quarrelled violently with Donnisthorpe, who then asked Isaac to pass on to Lister a "Black Letter" saying he considered Lister to be "a liar, thief and a rogue" and threatened to take him to court. Lister told Isaac he was willing to take on Donnisthorpe, 'I think I shall earn the character of a regular "Boxer at Law".' Twisting and turning Lister then proposed to raise money by admitting Donnisthorpe and his business partner, John Crofts, to a fifth share of Lister & Holden; Isaac reluctantly agreed to this provided it was in the form of a limited joint stock company. [The recent Joint Stock Companies Act of 1856 provided for limited liability for all joint-stock companies provided, amongst other things, that they include the word "limited" in their company name.]

Lister's cash flow problems persisted and he wrote again on 1st October asking Isaac to offer 'nominal security' for all his debts, estimating that he owed £160,000 (approximate to over £13 million in today's terms) to his creditors in Halifax over the next 12 to 18 months, and again raising the option of Isaac's buying his share in the French concern saying, 'I prefer to have less risk in France'. At the same time Lister was in dialogue with Tavernier; Angus warned: 'Tavernier is going swaggering that he is in again with Lister. That Lister invited him to Manningham Hall.'

Unconvinced that he had the capacity to meet his debts Isaac declined to act as surety for Lister. Lister even offered to sell him a share in his English business for £85,000. Isaac declined the offer but seized the moment to secure a deal to buy Lister's share of the French concern. The Memorandum of Agreement specified Isaac was to purchase all of Lister's shares in Lister & Holden together with Lister's French patents for £74,000 (equivalent to £6 million in today's terms). Lister retained the right to spin cotton, silk or flax in France. They signed the agreement on November 8th 1858. Isaac wrote to Sarah the following day announcing, 'I suppose I have bought the whole French business on good terms which I shall explain when I see you.' The final negotiation included Lister paying Isaac £11,250 to secure the release of Donnisthorpe and Crofts from the partnership.

Without doubt, after initially helping him, Isaac had taken full advantage of Lister's dire predicament in buying him out at advantageous terms. Although in the immediate aftermath their relationship was quite cordial, even friendly, perhaps unsurprisingly this gave rise to a deepening sense of grievance and animosity on Lister's part. On the other hand, Lister was pursing an alternate strategy, which may well have led to the sale of Lister's share to Donnisthorpe and Crofts, or even to Tavernier and the Baron de Fourment. Whichever combination had prevailed, this would undoubtedly have resulted in their taking control of the business that Isaac and his nephews had worked so hard to build.

Fearing the stress that work and the negotiations were having on his health, Sarah strongly urged Isaac to return to live in England. Isaac responded,

> *'I have been incessantly occupied from morning to night, till I am quite tired of it and want to run away from it as soon as possible. I quite agree with you in the main on all you say, but the lads must have a business and I prefer it should be in England'.*

During these fraught negotiations Isaac repeatedly shuttled across the channel arriving at Bradford on November 22nd from Paris, leaving on the 28th for London, making a night crossing to go to Lille where he was involved in a patent case on the 30th, crossing again on the night ferry two days later and arriving by train in Bradford to sign the Deeds the following day. He still found time to attend two chapel services at Eastbrook.

7. Isaac Holden et Fils

A snug little business of our own

Angus and Edward were immediately admitted as partners in the renamed business, *Isaac Holden et Fils*, but his nephews had to wait another decade before they were afforded a share. This was probably a bad move on Isaac's part as both the nephews had already proved their worth and he needed to reward their loyalty. He harboured strong doubts about his sons' commercial acumen, telling Angus:

> *'I fear much whether ever you (will) acquire those minutious and careful, painstaking habits which are necessary in manufacturing business; and as to Edward, I fear he will not only be seriously wanting in those respects but also in constancy and perseverance'.*

Angus, who had just turned 26, told his father, 'I should like us to be put in the way of a permanent business - none of these bubbles like combing- which will only last as long as there are patents to protect it – but a complete snug little business of our own.' This letter must surely have confirmed Isaac's misgivings; Angus had totally failed to grasp the commercial significance of commission combing as the business model, which underpinned the family fortunes for the remainder of the century and beyond. Later in the year, he had cause to reprimand Angus for drawing money 'very briskly' out of the business and begging him 'not to form expensive habits before

69

you are worth something', pointing out that his drawings that year had amounted to about as much as Isaac himself had spent on 'Furniture, education, living etc., for the family from 1849 to 1857.' Such lavish drawings, which were more than matched by Edward, must not only have galled his two nephews but also the other managers and supervisors who had risked all to come to France to work in his factories.

When Angus and Edward bought a mill at Penny Oaks in Bradford for £635 the following year without Isaac having seen it, they were worried that their father disapproved. Penny Oak was regarded by Isaac as his "experimental works" which he used to refine carding and washing processes as well as to continue investment in perfecting the Square Motion machine and trials with competing machines. He invested around £20,000 (£1.6 million in today's terms) in the experiments at Penny Oaks over the period 1860 to 1864. Honeyman and Goodman have shown that his control over the patents for the Square Motion machine in France led to widespread diffusion and sales to other manufacturers in every worsted-producing area in France.

Isaac wrote to another Bradford businessman, Bentham, in October 1860 advising him not to invest in combing in France, but to put his money into England. He correctly calculated that the newly signed Treaty of Commerce, the Chevalier-Cobden Treaty between England and France (negotiated by Isaac's long-term political hero, Richard Cobden, with the French economist, Michel Chevalier) would benefit the English worsted trade and this must have informed his decision to invest in the English worsted industry. Isaac had actually advised the French Council of State on the Treaty which reduced French duties on most British manufactured goods and reduced British duties on French wines and brandy. A "win-win" so far as Isaac was concerned because he (and his customers) were able to export combed wool and worsteds to France and to import a large amount of fine wine. In consequence the value of British exports to France more than doubled in the 1860s.

He was winding down the factory at St Denis so that he could use the profits accumulated there to grow the business in Reims and Croix, which were now more central to the French worsted industry. The factory at St Denis was finally closed in November 1860 and the machinery and some of the labour moved to his other factories in France.

My dear old machines

In 1860, Isaac became ill with a combination of fatigue, severe headaches and his old complaint of pulmonary asthma. Put under pressure from his doctors and Sarah to retire he began to plan to withdraw from the day-to-day management of the business and to pass over the running to his sons and nephews, whilst retaining a key strategic role as head of the firm.

When he moved back to Bradford and supposedly "retired" at the end of 1860, Isaac actually spent much of the next three years overseeing his businesses in France. He wrote to Sarah from Croix in April 1861 admitting that 'I do not seem quite like a man retired. It seems that when I come within the sound of my dear old machines, the old passion comes over me and I cannot keep aloof from them.' He promptly decamped to Reims, Paris and Alsace on a three-month business trip. After a short break in Scarborough he was back in Reims in September and October complaining that a young man he had sent out to join the firm from Keighley had not turned out as promised: 'An Englishman is worthless unless he is an accomplished French scholar.'

Civil War

The American Civil War had begun to have a serious economic impact on trade. The cotton supply was interrupted at first by a Southern imposed boycott and then later a Northern Union blockade. The Liberal Radical leader John Bright spoke out in favour of the Northern cause. Alongside other Liberal minded manufactures in Bradford Isaac was sympathetic to the Northern cause and wrote to a colleague in Rhode Island urging him to manufacture in the North to keep the economy afloat. Not all Liberal manufactures and politicians took the Northern side; the Liberal politician and textile manufacturer A.J. Mundella, backed the South because of its effects on his hosiery business in Nottingham.

In October 1861, Isaac and his sons contributed some £300 to the Bradford Relief Fund for the cotton workers. Perhaps this was enlightened self-interest; in terms of the scale of their profits this was a modest contribution given that it is estimated that some 400,000 workers were dependent on relief. Isaac was a supporter of the anti-slavery cause, but openly acknowledged the civil war had given 'a mighty stimulus' to the wool business, as muslins and cottons were replaced in the 1860s by grenadines, alpacas, lamas, soft cashmeres and twilled flannels. 'French ladies discovered that light woollens were safer to wear in the chill of the evening than muslin or cotton.'

The Alston Works

Isaac had ambitious plans in hand for expansion in Bradford, where he was having the large scale Alston Works built at Thornton Road under the supervision of his sons. Angus reported regularly to Isaac on the development:

> 'We shall have to decide when you come back about the height of the chimney. I was speaking to Mr. France yesterday and he thought that 30 yards would be rather stumpy and that was the height you talked about. The dye-works chimney by Fairbank's mill which has just been built is about 37 yards high and looks very well'.

The Alston works opened in 1864 and was managed by Thomas Craig. The experimental Penny Oaks factory was closed the same year. Twenty years later James Burnley wrote a description of the Alston Works describing the eight-acre factory as a 'model one'. The great shed alone occupied six acres, its stone floor 'reverberating beneath one's feet' with the sound of 117 gigantic carding machines and 150 combing machines. Employing 700 work-people:

> 'The carding machines are kept running night and day, two relays of work-people being employed. During the day both males and females "mind" these machines, but at night only males are allowed to work them. The combs, however, are such delicate instruments, and require such tender handling, that females only are intrusted with their management – male fingers are considered too clumsy to have the handing of them. Hence arises the necessity of a double supply of combs, since night labour for females is against the law'.

'In France, females work by night as well as by day, the same proportion of combs as at Alston Works is not required.' Isaac's papers show, for a 60 hour week at the Alston Works, men working in the combing room in 1864 were paid 16 shillings a week and women 9 shillings, by 1894 the men were paid 24 shillings a week and women 13 shillings.

Burnley describes the shed and workrooms as being roomy and well ventilated, and contrasts these 'model' factory conditions with the 'devil-holes' of close smelling and over–heated earlier combing factories. The Alston Works was supplied with its own water supply. A branch railway connected the works directly with the Great Northern railway system. Between them the French and English factories were now combing 31 million fleeces a year.

8. New Alliances

A joint marriage

Despite misgivings about his sons' abilities as businessmen, at no point does Isaac seem to have considered taking his daughters into the firm. His expectations were that each would become a 'Prudent Wife'.

A courtship between Mary Holden and Henry Illingworth formally began in June 1858 when Mary wrote to her father seeking his permission to the courtship. The ties between the Illingworth and the Holden families were then consolidated when Angus Holden became engaged to Illingworth's sister, Margaret.

The Illingworth's were an affluent Baptist spinning family. Daniel Illingworth, who had long been known to Isaac, died in 1854 leaving the Providence mill to his two sons, Henry and Alfred. They set up the Whetley Mill in 1865 and became one of the largest manufacturers in Bradford. [The firm of Illingworth were the last wool combers to use the Square Motion machine, which they continued to use until 1963.]

The two couples were married in May 1860, the brides wearing white moiré-antique wedding dresses with white tulle, tucked up with flowers and simple white bonnets. Mr and Mrs Henry Illingworth spent their honeymoon on the Isle of Wight and Mr and Mrs

Angus Holden in the Lake District. A light-hearted Angus wrote to Mary on returning from honeymoon:

> '*La! Turned half past 8pm in our squat little study – gas lit – window put down – raining pelting outside – Margaret sewing by my side, and all snug and right and tight. It is under such circumstances that Angus Holden of Bradford town sits down to pen what according to some prying circles would be called lots of moonshine which being interpreted means bosh*'.

Shortly after her marriage Mary wrote a frank letter to her sister on the subject of their stepmother, Sarah, 'Poor dear father, I do pity him that old creature, for I know he is miserable with her, he cannot be otherwise.' Angus had written equally frankly to Maggie saying, 'All much as usual St Denis the same dismal hole – old Madam just the same as she always was.'

There is an intriguing, but jocular letter sent on October 9th 1860 by the newly married Henry Illingworth to his sister-in-law, Maggie Holden:

> '*Have you forgotten "our" last drive to Paris in the Voiture de Ville, when (you) were the only witnesses of my – shall I call it – weakness? I have sometimes been inclined to think you would put down the scene as "far fetched", yet cannot but come to the conclusion that your own lovely nature would interpret it leniently as well as sympathetically*'.

Having married, Mary spelt out her expectation that her sister Maggie would now care for their father:

> 'You must be his greatest comfort and happiness when you leave school. You must consider it your duty to attend to him, cheer and solace him, now he is getting old'.

Gainsaying his strictures to his sons 'not to form expensive habits before you are worth something', Isaac made a substantial gift to both the new married couples to enable them to set up in large houses in Bradford. Henry wrote to Isaac thanking him for the gift, which had enabled him to purchase Lady Royde Hall. Angus and Margaret Illingworth were similarly lavishly set up at Daisy Bank.

When Edward Holden married Maria Wood he was treated with equal generosity. However, when his youngest sister, Maggie, married Alfred Illingworth five years later she wrote complaining to Isaac that she had not been treated fairly:

> 'I always was and always shall be a poor beggar where my own interests are concerned ... The first instalment [on the new house] is due on the first of next month and I do assure you that Alfred and I were not a little amazed when you told us you were not prepared to advance a payment for a few years, up to that moment you had always led me to expect that I should share equally with Angus, Edward and Mary.
>
> I am very sorry to be obliged to write such a letter, tho' you may easily imagine how these things preyed on my mind for I see no reason why I should be treated differently from the rest when I know you are so able to do for all alike'.

Chastened, Isaac subsequently instructed Angus, who was then handling his financial affairs, to pay £12,000 (just under £1 million in today's terms) to Maggie and Alfred.

In 1864, Mary was diagnosed with consumption and was looked after by her sister in Torquay for three months. Maggie wrote to Isaac telling him, 'The leeches applied on Mary's chest did her much good.'

Margaret was concerned about the state of the house at Oakworth, as she wanted to entertain guests on her return, and asked Isaac to 'have things boxed up a little.' In contrast to the rising aspirations of his children Isaac wrote to Angus Love, 'I still punish myself by my unconquerable desire to effect economies. How foolish it is to do so when one has enough to get through the world more easily.'

Oakworth House

Impressed by the magnificent chateau Isaac Crothers was having built in France, 'It is a fine building... I wish we had one in England', Isaac began to frame his own designs for rebuilding Oakworth.

Now an established member of Bradford's Millocracy, Isaac chose to mark his own rise to wealth by building a grand country mansion. This at a time in which the majority of Bradford's working class families lived in one room deep, back to back housing with one room upstairs and one downstairs with a windowless cellar with privy middens (a toilet system with a primitive pit for waste) serving several families. He took more than ten years (1864 to 1875) to build an elegant Italianate villa designed by the Bradford architect, George Smith, on the site of the former Sugden home at Oakworth. [George Smith also designed the magnificently restored Thornton's Arcade in Leeds, which was built shortly after Oakworth]. Italianate architecture was in vogue –Robert Kell, a fellow a wool manufacturer, completed his "Italianate-Baroque" villa at Heaton Mount in the mid 1860s designed by local architect J.T. Fairbank.

As an engineer, with an interest in the best that new technology could offer and an obsession with a healthy environment, Isaac was closely involved in all aspects of its design. He installed electric light run by plant on the premises and gaslight, and a telegraph and telephone linked on a private line to his children's homes. He believed that rooms should be kept at an even warm temperature and well ventilated. Central heating, double-glazing and air conditioning by means of inlets into each room and extraction of foul air by special ventilation shafts were also installed so that fresh air could be circulated every half hour. Three reservoirs and 7,000 feet of piping fed the radiators for the house, winter garden and glasshouses.

John Bright MP described Oakworth as 'a magnificent place, containing almost all that the heart of a man could desire, save a dog'.

The catalogue for the sale of Oakworth a year after Isaac's demise provides us with many of details of the house and gardens. A large portico, with an iron and glass awning for carriages to draw up in the dry, led through an oak panelled entrance hall into a central hall surrounded by a balcony with paintings by the contemporary artists. A corridor with busts by J. Adams-Acton of Isaac and of his heroes, Cobden, Gladstone and Lord Brougham, led to a drawing room in which the walls and ceilings were decorated by Italian and French artisans. The dining room, with a marble clock adorned with a bronze figure and two matching vases by Barbedienne of Paris, had a large bay window providing access to the winter gardens. Bronze busts by Barbedienne of Shakespeare, La Fontaine, Michelangelo, and Socrates embellished the richly panelled library with its light oak bookcases. A morning room, study or smoking room, and billiard room with a domed ceiling and oak fireplace completed the family rooms on the ground floor. The upper floor had eight bedrooms, a ladies boudoir, two bathrooms, and servants' quarters accessed by a secondary staircase. There were separate offices, kitchens, a butler's pantry, and wine and beer cellars. The house also boasted a Turkish bath and a billiard room as a gentleman's retreat next to the winter gardens. Isaac was a keen advocate of hydrotherapy and included taking regular Turkish baths as part of his fitness regime. The billiard room was the location of a speech made by John Bright on the Reform Bill on a visit to Oakworth in 1884.

Behind the house was winter garden covering half an acre heated by two furnaces so his reclusive wife, Sarah, could walk undisturbed in the winter months. The garden with its labyrinthine walkways and passages was adorned by French artisans with grottos and caves (made from concrete but given the appearance of limestone), and an array of waterfalls which Isaac could illuminate as his party piece for visitors with electric light generated by a gas engine. The half an acre of hot houses with their stained glass dome contained an orchid house, vineries, peach house, fig house and tomato house, providing all the year round fruit and fresh flowers, which Isaac had sent daily to London by train as gifts for his friend's and colleagues in the House of Commons. The nearby Oakworth School's record books also show that Sarah took the children oranges at Christmas.

The gardens were laid out with about a thousand yards of mosaic paving created by Italian craftsmen. There was an additional 30 acres of parklands with five miles of gravel paths. Isaac delighted in showing people round his grounds, which were open to the public at weekends and on public holidays, and became a major local tourist attraction.

A Methodist chapel stood immediately adjacent to Oakworth House. The house cost £80,000 (around £6 million in today's terms), with the grottoes, mosaic floors and the glasshouses and dome costing a further £120,000 (around £9 million in today's terms) to build. Over time Isaac extended his Oakworth Estate with the purchase of Highfield, Low Bank, Race Moor, Gill Clough and far High Field farms and a number of cottages.

Isaac's children were living in similarly lavish style as Angus Holden's accounts for 1871 indicate: Woodlands (Angus Holden's home on the outskirts of Bradford) - land £16,409, builders £28,940, furniture £5,069, pictures £4,792 – a total of £55,211 (more than £4 million in today's terms). In their book on Edward Burne-Jones, Victorian Artist-dreamer Alan Crawford and Laurence Des Cars cite an article in the Bradford Illustrated weekly of 1885 which refers to:

> '... the music room, added to the north-east end of Woodlands some years after the original construction was finished ... includes a large window containing in its upper compartment nine stained glass figures, the work of the celebrated artist Burne-Jones'.

Burne–Jones also created the four stain glass panels depicting the four seasons in the dining room at Cragside, the home of Sir William Armstrong. Angus had a substantial collection of paintings at Woodlands including the pre-Raphaelite, *Bride of Lammermoor* painted in 1878 by John Everett Millais.

Oakworth House was burnt down in 1906 and the house was demolished, leaving the stone portico as reminder of its former glory, and the caves and grotto. After some local controversy over the use of public money to create a park on the site, Sir Isaac Holden's grandson, Francis Holden Illingworth, who gave the land for this purpose, opened 'Holden Park' on May 25th 1925. The park has recently been restored with considerable local effort. Isaac's great grandson unveiled a blue plaque on the site of the house in 2012.

Photographs relating to Isaac Holden.

Sir Isaac Holden by Harry Furniss
National Portrait Gallery Image D121

Albert Sachs
20, MANNINGHAM LANE
BRADFORD.
PERMANENT CHROMOTYPE.

ISAAC HOLDEN
about 1885

MRS. ISAAC HOLDEN
about 1885

Sarah Sugden
Isaac's second wife

85

Back: Isaac Holden Crothers, Thomas Craig.
Front: Angus Holden, Isaac Holden, Edward Holden.
About 1882.

Alston Works Bradford

Holden et Fils factory, Rue Holden Croix

L. P. 12 - CROIX - Nord - Usine Holden

3. CROIX (Nord) - La Grande Cheminée (Hauteur 105m.) - E.C.

15 — Croix *(Nord)* - Rue Holden - Temple Anglais

OAKWORTH HOUSE

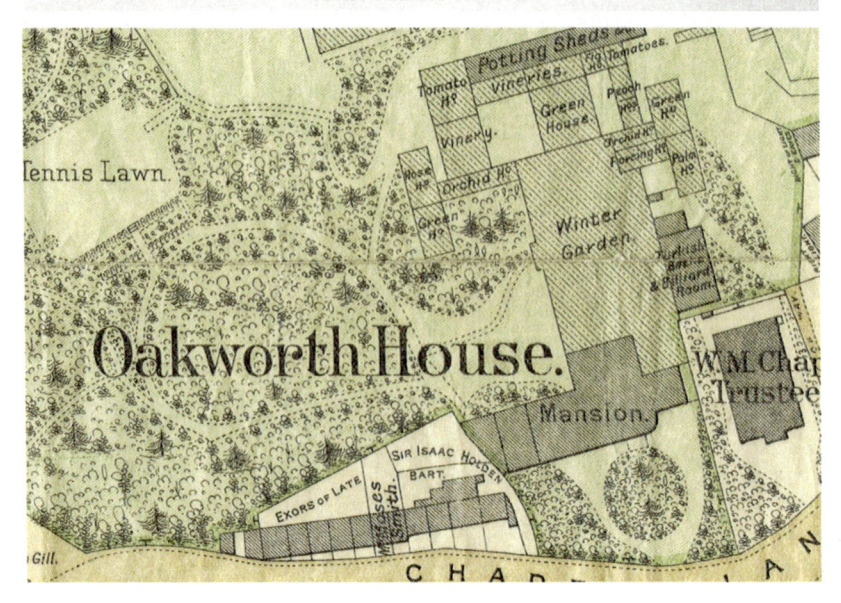

PRICE TWOPENCE.

THE SQUARE MOTION COMBING MACHINE:

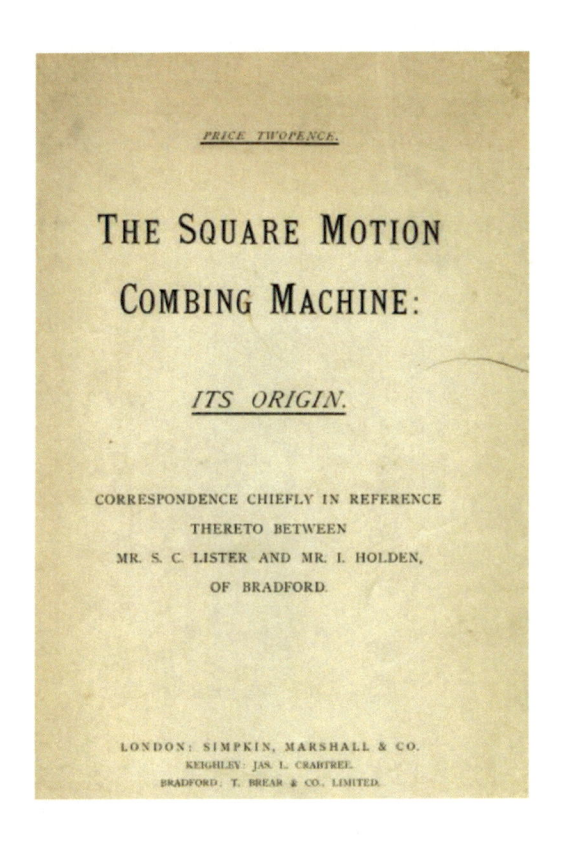

ITS ORIGIN.

CORRESPONDENCE CHIEFLY IN REFERENCE
THERETO BETWEEN
MR. S. C. LISTER AND MR. I. HOLDEN,
OF BRADFORD.

LONDON: SIMPKIN, MARSHALL & CO.
KEIGHLEY: JAS. L. CRABTREE.
BRADFORD: T. BREAR & CO. LIMITED.

Square motion comb in James Burnley 'The History of Wool and Wool Combing', 1889

Cartoon of Lister's statue drawn by Isaac

Photographs relating to Samuel Cunliffe Lister.

MR. SAMUEL CUNLIFFE LISTER.

Statue of Lister,
Lister Park, Bradford

Photographs relating to Angus Holden.

Angus Holden

Angus Holden

Photographs relating to Edward Holden.

EDWARD HOLDEN
about 1870

MRS. EDWARD HOLDEN
about 1870

Southport Glacarium

Photographs relating to Jonathan Holden.

Jonathan Holden

THE CHATEAU AT CROIX

Jonathan Holden's Chateu

Photographs relating to Mrs. Henry Illingworth (nee Mary Holden).

Photographs relating to Alfred Illingworth.

ALFRED ILLINGWORTH
about 1860

MARGARET HOLDEN
about 1864

Alfred Illingworth

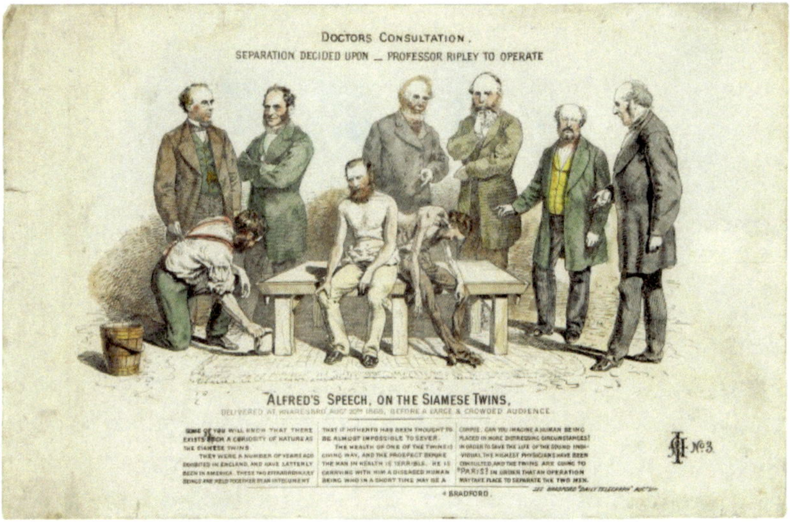

9. Dissenters Grievances

Conduce *most materially* to the work of God.
Returning to live at Oakworth at the end of 1860, Isaac was invited to join the Eastbrook Methodist Society. Doubtless already aware of his financial contributions elsewhere, the members of the society had a view to his fundraising capabilities; their invitation referred to Isaac being one whose support could 'conduce *most materially* to the work of God in the circuit.' It is interesting to note that Isaac did not elect to join the more prestigious Horton Lane chapel, which was known as the "Cathedral of Nonconformity" and spawned four of the first five of Bradford's mayors.

Isaac duly made generous contributions to the Eastbrook chapel, including building work in 1863, referred to in a letter from Angus:

> 'Eastbrook chapel is proceeding very satisfactorily and we shall have it ready in plenty of time for the opening ... we have secured one hundred voices of the Bradford Festival Choral Society to sing a few choruses and assist the choir, which you may be sure will be very fine'.

Inundated with requests for support from chapels, in 1863 alone he contributed £1500 to the Methodist Missionary Society and a further £300 to the Irish Jubilee Fund. Isaac and Sarah made substantial donations to the Wesleyan community in France supporting the chapel funds not only in St Denis, Croix and Reims, but also in Nimes, Côte d'Or and Calais where he frequently worshipped when travelling. He also gave long-term support to a seminary for training Methodist preachers at Lausanne in Switzerland.

A feeble voice has a chance to be heard

His return coincided with the creation of the Metropolitan Chapel Fund in 1861 to support the growing working class communities in central London. Isaac pledged £50 for every chapel in London with 1,000 sittings on two conditions: Firstly, that it did not follow the trend for high ceilinged "Gothic" architecture but was simple in structure and design so that, 'a feeble voice has a chance to be heard, and an ordinary voice to be heard with ease'. Secondly, he offered a further £50 if the trust deed contained a clause 'excluding forever the use of Liturgy' because it alienated the workingman. 'We want no better book of praise than the Wesleyan hymnbook.'

He was swimming against the tide in trying to resist the Neo-Gothic, 'Romish-Priest-architecture' style of chapel building, which became the dominant form by the 1890s. When the local wool trade consulted the leading art critic John Ruskin about plans for a new Wool Exchange in Bradford, which opened in 1864, Ruskin asked satirically:

> *'I notice that among all the new buildings that cover your once wild hills… the churches and schools are almost always Gothic, and the mansions and mills are never Gothic. Will you allow me to ask precisely the meaning of this? For, remember, it is peculiarly a modern phenomenon. When Gothic was invented, houses were Gothic as well as churches. . . . But now you live under one school of architecture, and worship under another. What do you mean by doing this?'*

Isaac was an original shareholder in the Wool Exchange. By 1871 he had subscribed £3,900 (around £300,000 in today's terms) to the Metropolitan Chapel Fund. Chapels in Bayswater, Bethnal Green, Blackheath, Bow, City Road, Highbury, Highgate, the Isle of Dogs, Kentish Town, Peckham, Stoke Newington and Wandsworth are amongst those chapels endowed by him in London. He became disenchanted with the momentum for large churches, which he feared:

> 'in their feeble imitation of the Establishment...
> (encourage) young people belonging to well-to-do-families
> ... to abandon Methodism and go body and soul to the
> fashionable religion of the established church and then
> possibly to Rome'.

He changed tack indicating he wanted to support smaller 'Meeting Houses' in London. This decision was partly prompted by Angus, who was looking after his financial affairs, and was alarmed by the increasing scale of his philanthropy at a time in which the Franco-Prussian war was having a strong impact on the French concerns. Sir Francis Lycett, the Chair of the Chapel Fund, wrote challenging Isaac's decision to go back on his pledge 'to subscribe to £5,000 for assisting in the erection of 50 chapels' and pointing out that he was 'glad to find that your losses are £40,000 less than Mr. Angus estimated them.' Isaac's response was to say, 'I think the best thing you can do in London is to increase the number of humbler Meeting Houses where the poor would gladly assemble to hear our excellent Local Preachers and I shall be glad to help with that. Of course they will neither be Gothic nor ritualistic.'

Dissenters Grievances

Isaac's entry into politics was informed by his nonconformist religious convictions. He also shared the individualistic outlook of the political philosopher Jeremy Bentham, who held that every man was the best judge of his own happiness and saw the responsibility of the legislator as being to give free scope to the intelligence and enterprise of the individual. Bentham vigorously attacked laws that sought to interfere with the free expression of religious belief and attacked the privileges of the landed aristocracy and of the Church of England. Isaac, who passionately shared these beliefs, later described the 'animus' of his life in politics as being – 'rights, liberty and independence'. He also adopted a largely laissez-faire Benthamite attitude to factory reform.

He had long shared alongside other Nonconformists a strong sense of injustice and resentment at the sway the Established Church held over national affairs. This sense of injustice had undoubtedly been heightened by his early experiences. The key "Dissenters' Grievances" which Isaac was to pursue in alliance with other entrepreneurial Nonconformist Radicals in the Liberal Party over the next 25 years, both as an MP and outside of parliament, were: Firstly, the abolition of Church Rates, which were levied for the upkeep of parish churches on all local households whether or not they were Anglican. Secondly, the removal of the ban on Nonconformists entering the University of Oxford or graduating from Cambridge, which effectively disbarred them from entering many of the professions. Thirdly, the Disestablishment of the Church - the withdrawal of special state patronage and control from the church, and in particular its stranglehold on education.

He also shared with other self-made men in the manufacturing industries, who were now beginning to assert themselves in political life, a deep resentment at the power of the aristocratic landowners who had protected their interest through the imposition of the Corn Laws which he had vehemently opposed as a younger man.

The Liberation Society

Isaac began to take part in the affairs of the Liberation Society founded by Edward Miall, a wealthy hosiery manufacturer and editor of *The Nonconformist*. In 1844 Miall had organised a national dissenting convention as a result of which the British Anti-State Church Association was founded. Miall cynically described the Established Church as "a stupendous money making scheme" carried out under the name of Christianity. In 1853 the Association changed its name to the Society for the Liberation of Religion from State-Patronage and Control, usually shortened to the Liberation Society. The Society aimed to encourage the selection of Parliamentary candidates who shared their opinions within Liberal Party constituencies. Their campaign also extended to blocking candidates of whom they disapproved (including preventing the Anglican worsted manufacturer Edward Ackroyd from standing as the Liberal candidate for Halifax in 1865). Isaac was to become a treasurer of the Liberation Society.

Alfred Illingworth also became a treasurer and then chairman of the Liberation Society and was set to become one of the leading Nonconformist Radical Liberal MPs. Alfred was a political insider, a Liberal Party activist who, together with his co-conspirator and fellow manufacturer, Robert Kell, thrived upon the cut and thrust of Bradford politics; Kell was the President of the Bradford Branch of the National Reform Union. During the American Civil War they played a prominent role in supporting the anti-slavery position of the Northern states and Isaac supported their campaign.

Isaac began to contemplate standing for parliament and was invited to do so following a meeting he had chaired in Pontefract in the summer of 1864. Maggie wrote to her father in July complaining on his behalf about:

'Those foolish people who have put in the Pontefract paper that you had accepted before you had been publicly asked goes very much against Foie (sic).... Alfred was saying last night that the Bradford elections cost Titus Salt £1,000 and he was very much annoyed at its costing so much as he had thought of its costing him £500'.

In the event Isaac decided not to stand in Pontefract.

Knaresboro' insists: Parliamentary Reform and the Knaresborough Election

When Gladstone first joined Palmerston's government in 1859, he opposed further electoral reform, but changed his position during Palmerston's last premiership, and in May 1864 Gladstone said that he saw no reason in principle why all mentally able men could not be enfranchised. Palmerston retorted, 'I entirely deny that every sane man has a moral right to vote.' When Palmerston went to Bradford to lay the foundation stone of the new Wool Exchange on 9th August 1864, working class leaders organised a protest and 'working men imposed silence upon themselves'. W. E. Forster made a speech at the banquet that evening, which Isaac Holden attended, in which he told the Prime Minister not to assume that 'their forbearance must [not] be taken as proof ... that they did not desire their political privilege'.

At a reform meeting in Bradford in December, which Isaac attended, Forster pointed to the deficiencies of an electoral system that permitted the three major industrial towns of Bradford, Halifax and Leeds with their population of 350,000 the same representation as the small towns of Pontefract, Ripon and Knaresborough with a combined population of only 23,000.

Knaresboro' insists

Knaresborough represented all that was rotten in the electoral system. Historically it was a 'burgage' borough, meaning that the right to vote was confined to the proprietors of certain specific properties (or "burgage tenements") in the borough; in Knaresborough there was no requirement for these proprietors to be resident, and normally the majority were not. This meant that the right to vote in Knaresborough could be legitimately bought and sold. The 1832 Reform Act extended the franchise to all who possessed or occupied a house of £10 annual rental. Small boroughs with between 2,000 and 4,000 inhabitants lost one of their two members but Knaresborough was one of the smallest boroughs to retain both its seats.

In the 1865 election the Liberal Party in Knaresborough needed a wealthy man able to challenge the town's entrenched interests. Isaac's friend John Crossley, whose brother was the West Riding MP, put forward Isaac's name for the constituency. Angus also encouraged Isaac to stand, 'You will see by the accompanying letters that Knaresboro' insists. Mr. Lord will call tomorrow if you will send the accompanying telegram. Will you consult Alfred if you see him?' Isaac stood for Knaresborough in a closely fought battle against the Tory, "Noisy" Tom Collins, "a jovial Yorkshire man of the horsey type". Knaresborough returned two members; Isaac and Collins were contending for the second place with Basil Wood being selected at the head of the poll as a Burgess.

The Tory candidates were threatening to evict any tenants who failed to vote for them. On the hustings Isaac declared that any man who tried to coerce their tenants in such a way 'ought to be tied to a cart and be publicly whipped'; he guaranteed that if any householder were to be evicted or lost their job because of casting their vote for him he would provide for them. One example was Robert

Dobson whom Isaac supported financially having 'lost all his work under Collins'. He also made several loans to business people in Knaresborough including Henry Stockdale (£980), Robert Corker (£200), and Mr. D. Lord (£1,000). Angus referred to these Knaresborough loans in a letter he sent to Isaac in 1873, 'We will have settled pretty nearly all of the previous Knaresboro incidents of this description… Here endeth the financial settlements of the ancient borough of Knaresborough.'

The election campaign pulled few punches. Noisy Tom Collins, on a brilliant blue poster dated July 6th 1865, warned his townsmen that:

> '… your Representatives, are opposed by a stranger, by a man whose best years have been spent in France…. He is a Liberal and he is rich --- or, if you like it better, he is rich and he will be liberal – therefore the legal advisers of the radical party (one of whim at least has "cogent reasons" for wishing to get hold of such a fat goose) have with infinite pains and trouble ferreted him out. We have heard some wonderful things in connection with this wealthy and talented Candidate, amongst the rest that "the eyes of all France (!!) are on Knaresborough." Perhaps nothing less than a French invasion will be our punishment if we refuse to send this Anglo-French mill-owner to the English House of Commons'.

Isaac's bright orange poster condemned the feudal control of the rotten borough:

> 'Shame! Shame! On the individuals, Men of Landed Property, who still continue as in Feudal times, to coerce,

> *and order their Tenants, and expect their Votes to be given in accordance with those orders'.*

Another of his campaign leaflets took the form of a black edged, embossed memorial card depicting a memorial stone engraved, *In Memory of Tom Collins*. Isaac seems to have been self-possessed and incisive at the hustings; when taunted with being a Wesleyan, he quietly replied that he was proud to be numbered among such a company of the best subjects of the realm.

In the absence of the secret ballot polling day was a very public occasion in Victorian times and was often marred by scenes of disorder and violence. A newspaper report describes the scene:

> *'Knaresboro' yesterday was the scene of the keenest contest which the recent election has produced... although there was a good deal of shouting round the polling booth as the electors arrived, yet there was a remarkable absence of scenes of personal violence... As everybody anticipated, the contest lay between Mr. Holden and Mr. Collins; and so close and doubtful was the fight that at no period of the day did either of them lead by more than 8 votes. At nine o'clock Mr. Collins was five ahead; at ten Mr. Holden was six in advance; at eleven Mr. Collins had a majority of eight ... and in the last half hour Mr. Holden again shot ahead and won by four votes....*
>
> *Altogether there would not be much less than 4,000 persons at the declaration. The Returning Officer, having obtained silence, said: "Electors of Knaresboro', I have to state to you the result of the poll. The number of votes given for Mr. Wood – 156, Mr. Holden – 127, Mr. Collins – 123.... Three cheers were then given to*

> *Mr. Holden and on entering his carriage the horses were taken out and he was drawn by a large number of persons through the principal streets of the town'.*

Knaresborough's Methodists were not shy in coming forward to claim their rewards for their part in his electoral victory. A deputation of Methodist Ministers and 'a number of our influential friends' asked to confer with him in January on what he might do in parliament to secure Nonconformist 'rights and privileges' and also asked 'to place before you our exact position as regards the heavy debts of our chapel property'. They went on to ask him to donate £3,600.

The campaign had taken it out of Isaac who continued to be dogged by bronchial illness and severe headaches. He went to Nice to recuperate and was still consulting doctors when he began to become active as a Member of Parliament in February 1866. His main priority was supporting the Reform Bill introduced by Gladstone in March. The Bill proposed a moderate extension of the franchise, giving the vote to £7 householders (instead of £10) and £14 tenants (instead of £50) in the county seats. The Bill was supported by the Liberal Radicals led by John Bright but opposed by a group of right wing Liberals led by Robert Lowe. As the historian George Macaulay Trevelyan observed in his Life of John Bright, 'Nothing but the gangway separated Bright and Lowe, the two champions who represented the forces of democracy and aristocracy'. John Bright mockingly referred to Lowe and his supporters as the 'Adullamites', an allusion to the Old Testament story of the Cave of Adullam, which housed 'everyone that was in distress … and everyone that was discontented.'

Maiden Speech and the Reform of 'Faggot' Votes

The Reform Bill also proposed a minor redistribution of seats with 63 to be grouped together - including grouping Knaresborough with Ripon and Thirsk - to return 22 MPs. At that time voting was restricted to those with an "interest" (i.e. property) in the constituency. If a landowner subdivided a single property into multiple units, and transferred the title of each unit into the name of a separate person, each titleholder could then register to vote. These "faggot voters" would vote according to the wishes of the original landowner. There was no requirement for a voter to be resident; the landowner and faggot voter might both reside outside the constituency.

Speaking as 'the representative of one of the condemned boroughs' Isaac made his maiden speech on the Reform Bill on June 1st 1866, recalling:

> *'When he was first applied to represent Knaresborough he refused, because he understood it was a corrupt constituency, but he was happy to say he soon found that he was mistaken, and…the liberal electors accorded him a loyal, honest, and hearty support. He looked on upon this measure as a moderate change – an extension of the suffrage consistent with an equally balanced representation of all interests and communities in the country… He might be mistaken, but nearly all the land was exclusively in the hands of the middle classes, whilst only one-half of the borough representation was to be given to the working classes. How could they suppose so small a share of the representation would give the working classes a preponderating influence in the House?'*

Two weeks after his maiden speech, the Conservatives and 51 Liberal 'Adullamites' voted against the Government on a "wrecking" amendment to Gladstone's Reform Bill. The Conservatives formed a government under the Earl of Derby with Disraeli its leading light. Disraeli took on the mantle of electoral reform and introduced his own Representation of the People Bill in 1867, which was to become the Second Reform Act. Isaac introduced an amendment on June 21st 1867 in a debate at the Committee stage of Disraeli's Reform Bill to prevent owners of land within borough boundaries from creating faggot votes by registering voters for 'sham' buildings with a yearly value of less than £5. In the debate he likened landlord coercion to 'vile serfdom' and went on to say:

> 'It was generally found that tenants holding land thought themselves obliged to vote in accordance with the opinions of their landlords, and nine voters had been deprived of their holdings for giving him (Mr. Holden) a free and independent vote. He did not fear the extension of the borough if the defect of the old law were amended, but he wished to prevent any voter from voting in respect of land alone with a sham building erected upon it to evade the law'.

The ensuing debate demonstrated the extent to which both parties were using faggot votes to circumvent the democratic process. In responding to Isaac's intervention, Sir Henry Edwards said, 'He knew the town of Knaresborough well, and at the present moment the late Member, as well as the present colleague of the hon. Gentleman, had a good deal of land within the borough which gave votes, as there were several buildings upon it of stone or brick having doors, and he dared to say windows also, that were occupied by cows and horses.'

Isaac's amendment was defeated on this occasion by 98 votes to 106. However the outlawing of faggot votes in the boroughs was carried into law as part of the Representation of the People Act (the Second Reform Act) of 1867.

On 22nd May 1867 Isaac was in the minority of just 73 MPs who voted in favour of John Stuart Mills amendment to enfranchise women.

Church Rates

The abolition of church rates was one of main planks of the Liberation Society:

> 'Why? Because we believe it to be unjust, —because we think that to employ the force of law for the purpose of compelling the whole community to support the religious ordinances and worship of a small part of the community, or at least of a section only, is a principle in itself prima faciê and palpably unfair'.

A devout Anglican, Gladstone nevertheless believed that finding a solution to the church rates question would enhance rather than diminish the security of the Established Church. In 1866 he co-sponsored a Compulsory Church Rate Abolition Bill, drawn up in consultation with Edward Miall, making church rate paying voluntary. Isaac spoke in the adjournment debate on the Bill pointing out:

> 'The Methodist churches raised annually a sum of £2,074,000 for the maintenance of their own religious institutions, and all these, he believed, would be glad to be rid of church rates. They contributed liberally and freely to the support of their own institutions, and they

> *therefore thought they ought to be relieved from any obligation to support the institutions of so wealthy a body as the Church of England'.*

The Church Rate Abolition Bill failed on this occasion, but Gladstone subsequently reintroduced a Bill for its abolition that was passed in 1868. Isaac also spoke in the Second Reading debate in 1867 on a Bill introduced by Viscount Amberley resulting from a public petition about permitting scientific lectures on a Sunday at St. Martin's Hall. The philosopher, John Stuart Mill, speaking in the debate had asked the question, 'If you prevent any but a strictly religious employment of the Sunday, the only leisure day which is possessed by the mass of working men, what happens? … One is to make the churches places of display, places of amusement and levity. The other is to make them places of boundless fanaticism.' Speaking after him in favour of relaxation on the Sunday observance laws, John Bright said that coming into the House he had asked one Member how he would vote, and he said, "I shall vote against the Bill because there are a lot of infidels at the bottom of it". In his speech Isaac protested against it going forth to the public that they legislated in the Commons on religious grounds:

> *'It was on broader grounds that the House ought to reject the Bill. Parliament was not called upon to prescribe the religious observances or opinions that any portion of the people should hold, but it was his conviction that the observance of a weekly day of rest was of the utmost importance to the people of England.… The present Emperor of the French issued a decree on this subject in 1852, and was doing all he could to limit the desecration of Sunday in France'.*

Gladstone's support for religious freedom stemmed from the threats he perceived the State posed to the Established Church, but he never endorsed the disestablishment cause. He rejected the argument put forward by Miall that establishment is 'in itself is harmful to religion', pointing to the fact that the majority supported the Church of England. In his authorised biography, The Life of William Ewart Gladstone, John Morley offers a classic analysis of Gladstone's behaviour, which puts into context his move from the Tory to the Liberal party, and his adoption of liberal reformist policies:

> *'Mr. Gladstone was at this time in his politics a liberal reformer of Turgot's type, a born lover of government, of just practical laws, of wise improvement, of public business well handed, a state that should emancipate and serve the individual'.*

Such individualistic sentiments might help to explain why, whilst always on the Radical Nonconformist wing of the Liberal Party and a supporter of disestablishment, Isaac admired Gladstone whose sentiments about good governance and the Benthamite emancipation of the individual he shared.

Keeping Tabs on Business

Isaac kept a close eye on his business affairs whilst serving as an MP. In April 1866, Isaac Crothers alerted him to the fact that his old bête noir Tavernier had lost a court case for infringing one of Isaac's patents. In a letter reminiscent of Isaac's own squabbles with Lister, Crothers wrote in May complaining that Angus Holden had been putting pressure on him to increase his remittances back to England.

A Family Affair

In 1867, Isaac gave up his seat at Knaresborough in favour of his son-in-law, Alfred Illingworth, who was angling for Isaac's support in securing a seat. He proposed that Isaac fight the newly created constituency at Keighley and had canvassed both Knaresborough and Keighley Liberals to test the water with them. Margaret was initially resistant to her new husband standing at this stage of his career and wrote to Isaac asking him to 'use your influence with him to *entirely abandon* any idea of entering parliament for quite ten years.' However by July she was actively engaged in her husband's campaign for Knaresborough, 'Mr and Mrs Miall are staying with us – party after party - meeting after meeting…how I wish I could live in a world without elections.' Alfred Illingworth won Knaresborough with a slim majority of just 15 votes. Isaac was selected in 1868 to fight for the Liberals in the Eastern Division of the West Riding but lost.

Alfred had also worked to get Edward Miall selected in a by-election in Bradford in November 1867. Alfred himself had declined to accept the nomination, writing to advise the Secretary of the Reform League that 'Mr Miall's presence in the House of Commons is found now to be a national want.' Isaac took the chair at Miall's crowded election rally at the Alexandra Theatre where Miall had set out the case for 'household suffrage, not hampered and restrained by the personal payment of rates, but pure and simple suffrage.' When Miall was defeated in this election Isaac again took the chair at his post election dinner at the Victoria Hotel in Bradford and raised a toast to Miall as 'the champion of civil liberty and religious equality.'

Miall's defeat in the by-election triggered Illingworth and Kell and other Radicals to form a new Liberal Association in Bradford with ward committees. Better organised they were able to secure the selection of Miall alongside W. E. Forster as the Liberal candidates in 1868. Forster was elected at the top of the poll, but Miall was again defeated, this time by Henry Ripley, a 'milk-and-water Liberal'. [Henry Ripley developed a model industrial village, 'Ripley Ville', near his works.] Angus Holden and Titus Salt Junior brought to court a petition for an electoral irregularity in Ripley's election. Ripley was found to have given his agent an unlimited bank account out of which £700 was used to keep 115 public houses open to supply drink to voters who would vote for Ripley – and his election was overturned. Miall was elected in the subsequent by-election, and to celebrate Angus Holden organised 'a grand demonstration in my park' at Woodlands at which a 'complimentary address… signed by 1,500 workingmen of Bradford' was presented to Miall.

Alfred Illingworth gave evidence in a similar election petition alleging refreshments were provided for campaign workers in W.E. Forster's election in Bradford. Alfred was alleged to have told the landlord of the Gladstone Arms in Brick Lane to let the people have plenty of beer, but the court ruled this was not corrupt as all of them had always intended to vote for Forster. [Bribery continued as an aspect of electoral politics. In 1886 Isaac was asked by Joseph Chamberlin to subscribe £250 to enable the Liberal MP, Jesse Collings, to fight a petition for corruption in his Ipswich seat. Whilst Collings was personally cleared two of his agents were found guilty of bribery and Collings had to resign.]

Frederick Engels wrote to Karl Marx about the election results in November 1868 asking, 'What do you say to the elections in the factory districts? Once again the proletariat has discredited itself terribly. ' Engels blamed the 'milk-and-water liberals' adding 'the small towns, the half rotten boroughs are the salvation of bourgeois liberalism.'

As a leading Wesleyan Liberal Isaac was called upon by his party leaders to give them support in the general election campaign. He was asked to speak on Gladstone's behalf on the Irish Church question in West Lancashire. He was also prevailed upon by Lord Frederick Cavendish to use 'your great influence with the Wesleyans' in order to persuade them to vote for his brother's co-candidate in Preston, Lord Edward Howard, a Roman Catholic. Isaac not only did so, but also wrote to the '*Watchman*", the Methodist newspaper, urging them to vote 'in favour of the Gladstone policy for the man who, in the House of Commons, would support that policy... not that I give preference to a Roman Catholic candidate – just the contrary – but I consider it would not only be folly but a wrong to return a candidate, be he Protestant or Roman Catholic, who would oppose the policy.'

The Radical leader John Bright wrote to Isaac in August 1968 asking him to sponsor the Liberal paper, The Star, to the tune of £2,000. His approach was not entirely graceful, 'I have given 25 years in Politics from August 1843. You have come later into the political field but you can help in addition with *some purse.*'

Journey to the Holy Land

In 1869 Isaac and Sarah made a journey to the Holy Land. They set sail from Marseilles on the French steamer the 'Moeris' bound for Alexandria with twenty first class and thirty second class passengers, spending a few weeks in Egypt, then going by Ismailia on the newly built Suez canal to Port Said and Jaffa, and on to Jerusalem, then through Samara to Damascus, Beirut and Constantinople. A seasoned traveller, Isaac brought with him a small armoury: 'a fowling piece, a rifle (breach loader) and a revolver and most things necessary for comfort and safety'. He also went armed with 'influential introductions in Egypt and Turkey from Lord Clarendon [the Foreign Secretary] personally, so that we shall have every respect and attention'.

The day before they left Cairo they met the Prince and Princess of Wales at one of the Viceroy's palaces. Sailing along the Nile Isaac found there was 'nothing to interest us except the wild fowl. Now and again we killed one, but they are left to float down the river.' Along the way they went to a *café chantant* and saw 'a fine looking dark coloured girl dance in a most peculiar manner' before going on to observe 'a perfectly naked man after ducks and geese with his long gun … This must be a godless fellow because the Mussulmen don't hunt as they are not allowed to eat game'.

They were riding as many as eight hours a day and Sarah had a couple of bad falls from a horse. Riding a camel from Assuan to Philae was 'a very uncomfortable affair…Bad as it is to ride donkeys for hours without saddles it is infinitely worse on dromedaries.' Back in Cairo Isaac wrote to his children telling them he was gratified by the outcome of the Bradford by-election petition, 'I hope it will be a good lesson the bribers and bribed and make it easier in future to get the right man'. He had learnt from his Doctor that one of Ripley's sons had been in Cairo and experienced an uncomfortable time, 'if all the Doctor tells of him be true…he richly deserves to have been a short time in purgatory'.

After climbing the Great Pyramid they were invited to a Grand Ball in Cairo at which the Viceroy and the Suez Canal builder, De Lesseps (cousin of Empress Eugenie), were present. 'Lesseps has the air of a man of great tact and ability which one would expect from the ability and indomitable perseverance with which he has hitherto conducted this gigantic undertaking.' [The Suez Canal was officially opened later that year.]

They experienced a terrible sandstorm before arriving at Jerusalem in a small party accompanied by some twenty-two horses and donkeys and a dozen men. Jerusalem's gates closed at dusk and it was becoming the custom for tourists to stay in large encampments at the Jaffa Gate, as the Prince of Wales had done when he visited the city in 1862. Sleeping in tents at the Jaffa Gate, Isaac extolled a 'delightful life it is with all roughness, inconveniences and danger'. Moving on to Bethlehem they met the young Marquis of Bute: 'he whose conversion to Romanism created such a sensation… He seems a most zealous pervert … goes round the churches on his hands and knees'. [The Marquis of Bute's conversion in December 1868, which had caused a scandal, was the inspiration for Disraeli's highly successful novel, *Lothair*, published in 1870.

On their journey to the Dead Sea they had passed in sight of the Cave of Adullam, which may have given Isaac pause to reflect on recent political events.

Arriving at Smyrna on the homeward leg of their journey the Consul advised them to take 'an escort of 40 men which he offered to furnish at small cost, as the while country is infested with two bands of desperate Brigands'. On arrival at Constantinople they received a telegram from Angus telling them that two of their grandchildren had Scarlet Fever and decided to hurry home.

Education Reform

A strong believer in technical education for workingmen, Isaac provided the funding to establish a number of Mechanics Institutes including, most notably, the Keighley Mechanics Institute. He was a close friend and confidante of the Liberal MP, Swire Smith, a worsted spinner in Keighley, who shared his concern that Britain was falling behind its international competitors. Swire Smith sat on the Royal Commission that examined technical education (1881–1884).

Isaac had worked out his position on secular education in his notebook in 1858, 'the logical way to solve the religious education difficulty…with 120 different and often conflicting religious sects is for the state to provide an efficient secular education and the different religions propagate at their own cost their various dogmas'. He was a member of the Methodist Education Committee and campaigned for his fellow Wesleyans to support a system of 'national education, supported by rates and national funds, of purely education, and separate religious teaching…to be provided by the various religious sects in the country'. He unsuccessfully pressed for a full debate on the education question at the 1869 Wesleyan conference. He became frustrated with the way in which the Wesleyan committees were dominated by the clergy rather than laity. In 1871 he wrote to the Reverend William Arthur explaining that he had not attended the preparatory committees for that year's conference, 'not as some insinuated to my son Edward that I am in a "pet" because I was defeated on the education question', but, 'If the object is to hear the expression of Lay opinion only then the speakers should be chiefly laymen'. He resigned from the Education Committee, writing that the meetings 'are a farce… The exhibitions of bad temper among the ex-presidents and of rudeness is too much for me'.

He opposed elements of W.E. Forster's failed Elementary Education Bill introduced in 1867. State grants to voluntary education societies had begun in 1833 the principal aim of the Bill was to fill in the gaps left by the voluntary societies by setting up school boards for those parts of England and Wales in that there were insufficient school places for working class children. Forster's Bill favoured religious instruction, which Isaac and other leading Wesleyans feared would reinforce the dominance of the Church of England in board schools.

Isaac favoured teaching in schools solely based on readings from the Bible. In his address to the electors of the Eastern Division of the West Riding on August 21st 1868, Isaac had declared: 'we may and possibly must adopt a secular and compulsory education system in order to reach all our youth and especially in the rural districts.' He was referring to the proposal to allow School Boards the option of offering denominational teaching in schools. One of the effects of the proposal was to give the Church of England control, particularly in 'single school' rural districts. When Forster introduced his second Education Bill in 1870 an Anglican Birmingham MP, Dixon, supported by Miall, tabled an amendment the effect of which was to prohibit all religious education in board schools. The Government made its rejection a question of confidence, and the amendment was withdrawn; but the result was the acceptance by Forster and Gladstone of the insertion of the Cowper-Temple Clause as a compromise forbidding the use of denominational formularies in the board schools and allowing parents to withdraw their children from religious education. Alfred Illingworth was a member of the recently formed National Education League, which campaigned for a universally free and compulsory system of secular education, and part of its deputation on March 9th 1870 to Gladstone and Forster. He felt the Cowper-Temple Clause did not go far enough, and successfully campaigned for a later amendment giving parents a timetable informing them when religious instruction would take place so they could opt out.

Forster's motivation throughout was to reconcile religious differences and secure universal elementary education, "I had no wish to injure dissent nor to do it any good, and I had no wish to injure the

Church nor to do it any good. I simply wanted to get the children to school". An independent thinker, who did not consider himself bound by the views of the more radical dissenters in his Bradford constituency, Forster had deliberately distanced himself from the Illingworth and Kell faction. Illingworth was to throw his efforts in the ensuing 1874 election into unseating him.

10. All for Glory: the Franco-Prussian War

Turning his back on domestic political affairs for the moment, Isaac's attention now became focused on the Franco-Prussian War and its consequences for his business interests in France.

On 19 July 1870, France declared war on Prussia. Concerned about the safety his nephews and workforce and the security of his business Isaac and his two sons quickly made their way to Paris where on a drive to the Bois de Boulogne, 'We saw very few carriages and very few people except those working on the fortifications and the curious looking at them'.

Two days later they reached Reims finding Jonathan Holden by himself having sent his family away for their safety. 'Being so near to Chalons there is great activity and excitement here, but business is still going on … and our works are running as usual.' [After its defeat at Gravelotte, the French *Army of the Rhine* had fallen back to Metz where it was under siege by 150,000 Prussian troops. The Emperor Napoleon and Marshal MacMahon had formed the new French A*rmy of Chalons* and were preparing to relieve Metz to rescue their besieged army. See map on following page.]

Amid the turmoil, Isaac still found time to attend the French Protestant church at Reims, where, Isaac informed Sarah, he had heard: 'an excellent sermon on the Good Samaritan. The object

THE FRANCO-PRUSSIAN WAR, 1870-71

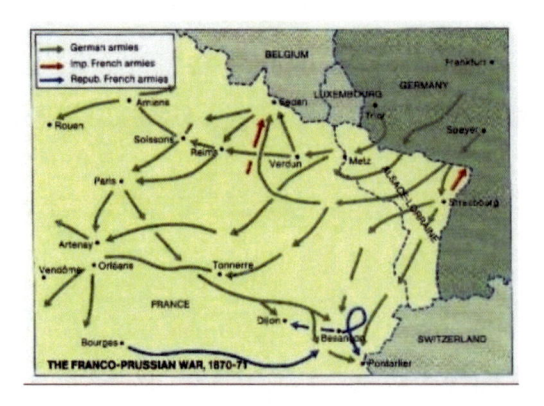

of the Minister was to prepare the hearts and minds of his people for the charitable duties they will likely have to perform from some terrible battle…No one knows when it will take place but the wounded will be distributed far and wide and they must be attended by some good Samaritans. How would you like to come and be a nurse?' He lightly reprimanded her for: 'making yourself into a hermit. I am doing nothing of the kind. We are out and about in the country and hear of incidents which will be something to talk about hereafter. Don't fear. I shall keep out of harm's way. We have here great commotion and formidable movements of troops of which it is not proper to speak at present.'

'There have been great military movements going on since we came' he wrote the following day:

> 'Today we rather expected to see a battle. The Prussians got within 5 miles, but great preparations were made to receive them, enough to make them turn away… We hope and believe the French army will be victorious at Metz…. All the English women have left or are leaving with four exceptions. They think it an opportune moment to visit their friends in England'.

[The Siege of Metz by the Prussian forces had started on August 19th and ended in their taking the city at the end of October.] On August 29th the party moved on leaving Jonathan and 'our affairs in the care of kind providence'. Two days later they had arrived back in Croix via Paris, where they had stopped off to renew their visas noting: 'Paris is in a state of terrible excitement. All foreigners are hurrying out of it.' Isaac reassured Sarah that he did not think the English women would be in danger in Croix. [Croix is located just outside Lille, which became one of the main bases for the French army. At that stage Isaac did not know that there had been a terrible battle at Sedan on September 1st with 17,000 Frenchmen killed and wounded and 21,000 captured. On 2nd September, Napoleon III surrendered himself and the entire *Army of Châlons* to the German chief of staff, Moltke. When news reached Paris of Napoleon's capture, a *coup d'état* took place and a new Provisional Government, effectively a triumvirate comprising Gambetta, General Troche and Le Favre, was installed.]

On September 4th the Prussian troops entered Reims and two days later the King of Prussia, accompanied by Bismarck and Moltke, made an imposing entry, and resided for some time at the episcopal palace, in the apartments reserved for the Kings of France at the time of their consecration. The special correspondent of the *Standard*, embedded with the headquarters of the King of Prussia, wrote an article from Reims on 10th September (published in the Leeds Mercury on September 20th), which provides a remarkable insight into the effects of the German occupation of the city:

> *'When the Germans first arrived, the Marie was anxious to assist their labours by quartering their men on the town by allotting them in the same proportions as his fellow countrymen, when a French army passes through*

127

Reims. But that particular offer was refused, and the city has been divided into so many sections, all having to bear a like burden... To show you how the system works, I will detail you a leading case that has come under my own personal observation. There is on one of the outskirts of this city a large wool-combing establishment – indeed the largest in the place. It belongs to an Englishman, whom I need designate no further than by saying he is ... cousin of the sitting Member of Knaresboro...The works here employ 1,200 men and I scarcely need add that the proprietor is a British subject. Last Sunday there came to him – and I speak of him individually, and not of his hands, who, of course, have had to bear their own burden in their own homes – the first batch of German troops. They consisted of 100 hussars and their horses. They left the following morning. To them, on that day at 2 p.m., there succeeded 250 men of an infantry regiment, four officers, and four horses....On Wednesday, after they had gone, there arrived 37 men and 100 horses. Moreover, his two private carriage horses were seized, and an outbuilding in another quarter of town (filled with hay and straw – his entire provision for the winter) was broken into without any proper and formal requisition. All these facts I had from the proprietor himself. He is, however, a gentleman of much spirit, and he declared that as long as no actual injustice is done he desires nothing better than to throw in his lot with the people amongst whom he lives and thrives. The wish nearest to his heart is to get a free pass for the wives and children of some of his English hands to the nearest point whence they could start for their own country. I ventured to say *that I could manage this for him, and also obtain any redress for the wrong he had suffered'.*

The special correspondent, who had clearly had access at the very highest level in the Prussian King's entourage, attached to his article a copy of a letter written in English by 'a person of great eminence' (a Prussian, hence the grammar):

'Dear Sir, The paper by Mr. H., which you gave me last night, I have immediately laid before his Excellency, who has given orders to his cousin, Count Bismark-Rholer, to apply to the État-Major for the permission requested by Mr. H's so noble and human a feeling; and to try also and find out where the fault of the apparently just grievance of Mr.H lies, and to procure redress, if possible'.

He concludes the article by referring to his trying to secure Jonathan Holden a pass to travel to Paris to release money to pay the wages. The pass was duly secured and on his journey to Paris on September 15th Jonathan wrote a hurried note to Isaac describing how on his journey over the Prussian lines and battlefields of Sedan what he had seen: 'surpasses in horror and misery anything of which I have ever read…. the people actually starving, all taken by the Prussian devastating army. At Sedan…all that can leave are crowding the roads with what they can carry with them'. In his absence he had left, 'a *Council of Regence* composed of all our principal men to confer daily upon all affairs and events … All the concerns in Reims are actually paying wages with small paper notes of their own making or all would be stopped'.

In a further despatch that appeared in the *Hull Packet and East Riding Times* on September 23rd the correspondent revealed that 'Mr. H' was 'Mr. Jonathan Holden':

129

> 'When I tell you that he pays some seven or eight hundred pounds every week in wages you will have some of the difficulties he has to overcome. He has in stock a certain number of five franc pieces, but no smaller specie. He is issuing his work people little "notes" of his own, of one, two and three francs, which are readily accepted by the shopkeepers of the town on the understanding promulgated by him that when anybody presents his "notes" to the value of three francs, plus two francs in specie, they will be exchanged for a five-franc piece'.

The correspondent described the restaurant on the Jonathan's works premises, which provided a morning meal for ten centimes and 'a dinner of substantial character' for three pence, but 'In no case can an individual have more than one glass of beer at a meal'. 'Since I was fortunate enough to bring his case before Count Bismarck, and to obtain from him what he so much desired, he has been emboldened to ask for permission to buy and house a large quantity of flour for the autumn and winter for his hands; and the permission has been immediately conceded.'

On September 26th Isaac Crothers wrote telling Isaac, 'there is great distress in Roubaix'. However, by the beginning of October he was able to reassure him, 'We are still working night and day… our customers are mostly all paying us but in bills at 90 days'. Jonathan had been to see him in Croix and 'hates the Prussians with perfect hatred'.

At the end of October Isaac went to Sedan and saw 'the frightful traces of war.' Jonathan wrote to his cousin, Angus Holden, on November 8th having torn up a letter he had previously drafted because, 'I had gone into the deplorable state of the present strife too fully'. His final draft expresses his fear that 'we are drifting to a deadlock'. He tells Angus about food hand outs which are 'liberally given to 13,000 persons (in Reims) which number is ever increasing by works stopping'. Jonathan now had the Prussian, Captain von Blucher, and his squadron forcibly billeted in his house. Jonathan was now forced to 'lead a most strange and monotonous life, no letters, no clients, no night work, scarcely any day work.'

Days later Isaac Crothers wrote to Isaac about the desperate position of the French armies asking, 'What do you think of Mr. Gambetta's new feat of calling out (up) all the married men – everybody –a l*evee en masse?* ...It will take about half our combing overlockers but a thousand times worse than that – it will take away hosts of our customers'. [The Prussian army besieged Paris during the winter of 1870-1871 and Gambetta himself had fled Paris in a balloon.]

On November 11th Jonathan reported the German troops had withdrawn from Reims but French soldiers had yet to arrive. 'The *franc tireurs* continue to give much trouble to the German troops around Megiere... our Captain von Blucher...has finally left this morning for Orleans, where he tells me they have had a defeat but are determined to repair it with a great force as usual.' He had just paid nearly double for coal supplies to keep the factory working, but had been told by the Sous Prefet that there was no hope of fresh supplies because the railway was 'being taken up with war material'. 'War is now raged against the people most bitterly.'

Jonathan paid a brief visit to Bradford in December 1870 and met entire families with little children fleeing from Amiens' on his return journey at Calais. Arriving at Lille he found 'the most complete ignorance prevailed on the state of the armies.' He went to Croix and 'got the amount of our Bills in notes' before becoming snowbound; the icy winter conditions had completely stalled their coal supplies that were coming by boat. Arriving back home in Reims Jonathan observed, 'Prussia is bent upon ruining France completely and leaving nothing but famine and civil war behind them.... We still have 8 Prussians in the house.' Later he wrote to Angus expressing his hope that 'in the future the two peoples will see their true interest otherwise than in the deadly strife or death struggle that now brings them together.'

Paris surrendered to the German siege on January 18th 1871 and an armistice was signed on January 28th. Some 30,000 German troops remained garrisoned in Paris until terms for their withdrawal were ratified; the Kaiser reviewed his troops at Longchamps as they marched out of the city on March 3rd. However, as a letter written by Jonathan to Isaac Crothers on March 6th indicates, the Germans continued to control all of the railways, 'All our railways are still entirely in their hands …the town is still full of their troops…they still hold all with a high hand.'

The German victory had cost them the lives of more than 28,000 men. When the French government was finally forced to surrender, a new government – *la Republique sans les republicans* - led by President Thiers was established at Versailles. Thiers ordered the army to remove cannons in the possession of the Paris National Guard and this led to the Paris uprising and the formation of the Paris Commune on March 28th. The Communards took to the barricades when the provisional government's troops began the re-conquest of the city on May 21st. During the last week of May, the '*Semaine sanglante*' ("The Bloody Week"), the Communards were brutally suppressed, between 20,000 and 30,000 Communards were killed. A final peace treaty was signed with the newly united German States on May 10th 1871. However this was not the end of the affair, Jonathan wrote to Isaac Crothers on June 2nd exclaiming:

*'After what has passed during the last two months ...
you may well feel anxious about the present and ultimate
position of poor unfortunate France. Her trials and
difficulties come and go with each day.*

*Our principal preoccupation is still transport. We have
with much labour and trouble got apart from Boulogne
where we still have several thousand bales... today we are
informed from Boulogne by telegraph that by German
orders nothing more can be forwarded... we are just
living from hand to mouth.*

*What can you call this? Are we still at war? It appears to
me that the Prussians are bent upon the ruin of French
industry. What can the Government be doing, have they
no authority I often ask myself '.*

Jonathan Holden bore the war with considerable ingenuity and fortitude and must be afforded the last word on the war and its consequences. On 27 July 1871 he reported to Isaac:

*'Estimate profits for the year ending 30 June 1871 at £
359,859.25, so that "Glory" has cost us a round million...
Albeit our position is better than that of those poor devils
who are slaves of Centralization and who must needs go
and have their bottoms pricked with bayonets, and their
heads smashed with fragments of shells and lie neglected
to die of misery and want, then robbed and buried and
be dead men out of mind – all for "Glory"'.*

11. Return to the fray: infidels and secularists, and spoliators

Returning to domestic political affairs in January 1872, Isaac was nominated in the forthcoming by-election as the Liberal candidate for the Northern division of the East Riding beating Henry Ripley to the nomination. In a speech made at the hustings in Halifax on January 24th Isaac described himself as "no orator"… My work has not been to make sentences but…mechanical…I cannot pretend as a mechanic, as one who has risen from being a mechanic with hard hands – I cannot pretend to perfect perspicuity in my language, but generally succeed in making people understand what I mean." However he turned a neat phrase: "We (nonconformists) have been much maligned. We have been called infidels and secularists, and spoliators, and many other hard names, but after all we are harmless people."

His old sparring partner, Lister, who was a Tory, intervened in the election by writing a detrimental letter about his claims to have invented the square motion combing machine (published in the Bradford Evening Mail on January 31st 1872). Isaac's solicitor responded in a letter challenging Lister to go to the arbitration on the question and that whichever lost should donate £5,000 to charity. Lister's unsought for intervention reignited their claims and counter claims that were to return to the public arena over the next two decades. Isaac sought a barrister's opinion as to whether he could sue Lister over the letter, but was told this would be ill advised given the 'temper' of the electoral climate in which it was written. He wrote to Donnisthorpe complaining that, 'My old partner, Mr Lister, seems to be somewhat envious of my prosperity and had been, as you are aware, disposed to throw dirt at me'. Isaac went on in this letter to reiterate his claim for perfecting the Square Motion and asked Donnisthorpe 'to give me the credit of it'. Maggie Holden wrote on 27th February advising, 'Father if ever your mind is troubled with thoughts of Lister turn for fortitude to the 37th Psalm and you will be strengthened. It is always what I do when I feel naughty on the subject…'

He also wrote in April to Lister declaring: 'your dishonourable conduct warns me to avoid (further) correspondence with you'.

Isaac was narrowly defeated at the poll on February 8th by Powell, the Tory candidate, who secured 6,961 votes to Isaac's 6,917. [Lister was nominated alongside Powell as the Tory candidate for the Northern Division of West Riding eight years later in 1880 but lost to the Liberals, Lord Frederick Cavendish and Sir Matthew Wilson.]

Isaac continued to be politically active outside parliament: In May he presided over the annual meeting of the Liberation Society; on September 9th he spoke at the inaugural meeting of a branch of the Reform Union; in September he was voted on to the executive of the National Education League and spoke at its annual meeting in November, where, dissociating himself from the official position of the Wesleyan Conference, he declared 'he was ready, for his part, to adopt a system of national education in which religious teaching should not be given'. In February 1873 he was campaigning for temperance 'against the drink habits of this unenlightened 19th Century'.

However he was not without his detractors. The columnist for *The Graphic*, in a brief profile of Isaac published on September 14th, noted:

> '*Though he seems to be an attractive speaker on the stump, he never that I recollect spoke in the House, and yet, whilst I write a dim, misty vision of him upon his legs comes to my mind. Mr. Holden is what is called an out-and-out Radical... In a speech which Mr. Holden delivered lately he denounced the institution of the aristocracy*'.

In January 1974 Isaac was selected to represent the Liberal Party for the Eastern division of the West Riding. This time his opponents branded him as being 'a supporter of godless education' who would 'exclude the bible from their schools.' Isaac and his moderate, Church of England, co-candidate, Sir John Ramsden, addressed as many as 14 election meetings a week during the campaign. Ramsden, who was a good orator, led the campaign and found himself defending Isaac, of whom some people had been asking, "How can you support such a rabid Nonconformist?" to which Sir John answered dryly 'he had been travelling with him these last ten days, and had seen no signs of him being "rabid" in any way'. Isaac and Ramsden lost the election.

Alfred Illingworth, who had stood down from his Knaresborough seat, used his energies in an acrimonious campaign for Miall's selection in Bradford and against the selection of W.E. Forster. The campaign centred on Forster's perceived failure to adopt the dissenters' views within the Education Act. In the selection meeting a disingenuous Illingworth, who had organised the anti-Forster caucus, urged those present "to distinguish between faithful servants and those who had lost that character" and went in to attack Forster's Education Act. After the meeting chose to adopt a stonemason, James Hardacker, Illingworth was attacked in the local press for dividing the Liberal party. The politically astute Forster then announced he would stand anyway and, when the Conservatives backed him and Henry Ripley, they were both elected. The Liberal party was defeated in the General Election of 1874.

Holden's Ghosts and the Wages Fund

In common with many other Liberal Nonconformist entrepreneurs Isaac was radical in matters of electoral and education reform, but generally reactionary when it came to workers rights and factory reform. In August 1872 he formed, alongside Sir Titus Salt and Co., part of a 'deputation of masters' to the Home Office to oppose the Nine Hours Bill introduced by the Liberal hosiery manufacture, A.J. Mundella, which cautiously proposed to reduce working hours in the textile industry for women and children from 60 to 54 hours per week. The "masters" spokesperson, Captain Shepherd, argued that as wool and worsted manufacturers they did not consider current hours to be excessive, 'the bulk of employers had conceded one hour on Saturdays, making a week's work 59 instead of 60, and most probably another hour would be granted'.

Isaac readily subscribed to Adam Smith and David Ricardo's *Wages Fund* theory, which held that capital supplied a fixed total of revenue for the remuneration of all workers, and that therefore, there was an inevitable reduction in the share for each as more workers were employed to take part in the division. [There is of course no such limited 'fund', which can be separated from other funds used in production. The 'fund' is a matter of the employer's discretion as to how much they would provide for wages.]

The wool combers in Isaac's factories typically worked a 60-hour week, often in conditions of up to 120 degrees Fahrenheit of heat in the combing rooms. In 1864, men working in the combing room at the Alston works were paid 16 shillings (£0.80) a week and women 9 shillings (£0.45). By 1894 wages had increased by about a third for men, but they were still earning almost twice as much as women. Women would often work to within one week of childbirth and return to work within a fortnight. Many of the male night workers, often called 'Holden's Ghosts' by people in Bradford, were employed on a casual basis having to attend each evening even if there was no work that night. Fred Jowett, described the wool combing workers' terms and conditions as a form of 'white slavery', because of their causal employment and low pay.

Asked about a campaign for an eight-hour day for coal miners in the 1890s, Isaac was still adhering to the Wages Fund theory:

> *'It would be our ruin – at least until the Germans and the French, our greatest competitors, reduce their hours… An hour's work a day may give the manufacturer his profit. If that is given up, it would mean the capitalist's profit is gone, and with it the labourer's wage is gone too'.*

However he went on to explain, 'In the case of the miner there is a danger and there is injury to health. They are shut out from the light of day. The more their hours are limited the better.' This may have reflected the fact that his father had been a miner.

Perhaps surprisingly the Holdens, Illingworths and Salts were at this stage still seen generally as being sympathetic to trade unionism. Alfred Illingworth was amongst the group of 101 Liberal MPs who voted against giving unions the right to picket in 1872, but lent his support to the agricultural workers union during a lock out in Lincolnshire in 1874.

Isaac later explained his own position to the Bradford Observer:

'Employers, he thought, do very foolishly in refusing to accept the intelligent picked men of the various trades as deputations or representatives of their interests. These were the men they should get hold of and negotiate with, as they were the most amenable to reason, and if convinced of the reasonableness of the master's representations, would have the most powerful influence on their fellow workmen'.

Honeyman and Goodman have noted his French factories at Croix and Reims had fewer incidents of industrial action than others in the area 'and negotiations over wages and other aspects of working conditions were quickly completed'. However French wages were generally lower than in England.

"Saunterer", the correspondent of the Bradford Observer, wrote two articles in June 1875 'On French Provincial Life', which provide a further insight into the pay and conditions, and gender inequalities of Holden & Sons French factories. Saunterer concluded that cheap labour gave French manufacturers a competitive advantage over their English counterparts:

'In England mechanics will earn 28 shillings for a week of 54 hours; at Lille good fitters and turners, for a week of 66 hours (6 days of eleven hours) get about 28 francs and 50 centimes, equivalent to £1 and 3 shillings in English. Overtime, which in England is "time and a quarter" ... in France does not count at any greater rate of payment than the ordinary hours of work'.

Following his visit to Reims Saunterer graphically described working conditions for women:

> 'There were the same beautiful machines that I had seen in operation at the Alston Works at Bradford but the workers were altogether different. The machines were almost entirely minded by girls, the majority of whom were shoeless and stockingless, besides being scantily clad in other respects. There was nothing in the least suggestive of immodesty about this, however, for the girls certainly behaved very decorously… Combing sheds are rather high in temperature, and the French girls adopt every available means of keeping cool. They come to work neat as can be … but as soon as they get to the side of their machines they divest themselves of their shoes and stockings and anything cumbersome in the way of upper garments.
>
> There are some 1,000 to 2,000 workpeople employed by this firm altogether at the Reims establishment, not more than a tenth of whom are English… nearly all occupied in superior positions, a large proportion being employed in the mechanic's shop… They have the advantage of good wages, of having their families around them, of comfortable homes to be in'.

Wages Fund theory was a convenient justification for low wages compared to the vast profits earned by many 19th century manufacturers. Honeyman and Goodman have calculated that in 1874 Isaac's factory in Croix employed 1,785 people and paid £1,500 a week in wages. Isaac's accounts show his personal net income that year was £91,982 (equivalent to around £7 million today), so he was earning more per week than all his employees at Croix put together. His investments at that time were worth more than half a million pounds (£19 million in today's terms). Additionally his two sons and two sons-in-law each drew £20,000 (equivalent to around £1.5 million today) as their share of the profits in 1874.

Despite living in opulence at Oakworth Isaac continued to promote to a credulous press what had by now become the myth that he lived an entirely simple life.

The unveiling ceremony for the 23 feet high statue of Samuel Lister at Manningham Park in Bradford by W.E. Forster MP on May 15th 1875 was to reignite the old enmity between Lister and Isaac. In his speech at the banquet that followed Lister made disparaging remarks about Isaac, 'a gentleman whom a great many thought he not like'. Lister said that Isaac 'had not given a valuable

Statue of Lister, Lister Park, Bradford

141

machine to the wool trade, and that if I was not an inventor, the New Zealander of the future would say that the statue was put up to the wrong man', and went on to deride his claims to inventing the square motion machine.

An irate Isaac took up the cudgels by responding to these allegations in a letter to the Editors of the *Leeds Mercury* published on June 10th suggesting that Lister's aversion to him was 'prejudiced either by interest, vanity, or caprice'. Lister's response printed in the *Leeds Mercury* expresses 'surprise and regret at Mr. Holden's long and angry letter' and goes on to pour scorn on Isaac's claims, made to the House of Commons Patents Committee, to have invented the Lucifer match, 'a matchless story'. On July 8th he wrote again to the *Mercury* challenging Isaac's presentation of himself at the 1872 election as, 'an ingenious, hard-working, self-made inventor – or in other words "a hard-handed mechanic" – whereas I know that he was only a soft-handed bookkeeper'. Lister was outraged that, 'He had got my French concern and the square motion which belonged to me, and derived immense wealth from them; and now he was claiming the credit of having invented the square motion'. In a further letter to the *Mercury* Lister claimed Jonathan Holden was responsible for getting the square motion machine working productively in France and that he had been the one who trained him to do so.

'Mr. Lister is the victim of an ungovernable jealousy', Isaac claimed in his response published on August 19th. Isaac quoted a letter he had written to Lister on December 25th 1851 in which he had said:

> *'In reference to the square motion, permit me to remind you of facts which you may have lost sight of - First, the employment of a finer circle that was then used – that*

in intended employing those of 16 per inch, laid aside as impractical by Mr. Ambler [Lister's other business partner]. Secondly, a very fine working comb entering the wool close to the circle from below and returning horizontally'.

More significantly Isaac recalled: "The morning after this conversation you informed me that you had written to Carpmael to take a patent for the square motion. I claim therefore much of the credit of its origin."

Isaac then turned to being charged by a haughty Lister with 'the awful offence of being represented in the catalogue of the Royal Academy as "the inventor of the combing machine".' This refers to a medallion bust of Isaac by Adams-Acton submitted to the Royal Academy in 1871 to which the artist had added this inscription without Isaac's knowledge. Isaac points out that he had reacted on hearing about the inscription, (actually through a letter written by Lister at the time), by asking for the inscription to be withdrawn in all future editions, 'What a pity Mr. Lister has not patented all pictorial illustrations, and thereby secured their exclusive me!' [Adams-Acton exhibited at The Royal Academy Summer Exhibition in 1877 a life-size white marble sculpture depicting Miss Holden, Isaac's granddaughter Annie leaning against a deer. The sculpture came for auction at Summers Place in 2013 with an estimated price valuation of £50,000-£80,000]

The last word on this round of the demeaning public altercation between the former partners goes to the Editor of the *Bradford Observer*, which had also been publishing the correspondence. He had received a letter from Lister demanding an apology from the paper for having published Isaac's last letter. The Editor comments wryly, 'Mr Lister must strangely misunderstand the relation of the press to its correspondents. When gentlemen append their names to their communications, they, and not we, are answerable for the accuracy of their statements'.

This is not the only time that the Victorian passion for the erection of statues stirred controversy. There is a cautionary footnote sounded by John Bright at the unveiling of the Cobden statute at the Bradford Exchange on 26 July 1877 at which Isaac presided. Bright declared himself as being one of those who were eager to promote statues as there 'were few men so conspicuous as to deserve them, and those who deserved them most certainly required them the least'. He quoted Eupolis' Hymn to the Creator, translated from the Greek, which asked:

> *Why need we monuments supply,*
>
> *To rescue what can never die.*

Paltry tricks

Having left the running of his businesses in France to his two nephews, Isaac was to be made increasingly aware of their rivalry. They were disputing their share of the partnership deed drawn up in 1872 by which Jonathan was divested of any involvement or share in the business at Croix but was made a partner in the Reims business for 12 years and awarded 'one-fifth of the capital profits'. It appears that Isaac Crothers was awarded a lesser share.

In 1875 Isaac Crothers complained that Jonathan Holden was continually haranguing Isaac and his sons with complaints about him and asked Isaac to arbitrate between them. Isaac sent Angus to hear both sides of the argument, a heated meeting in which he was described by Jonathan as having been, 'dignified and never spoke but to the point and the subject for which we met'.

The rancorous exchange of letters between the two nephews is reminiscent of Isaac's own conflict with Lister. One party or the other deliberately copied many of the letters to Isaac Holden in an attempt to elicit his sympathy. Jonathan wrote to Isaac Crothers on 17 March, 'Now be advised by a friend not to play such paltry tricks in writing such letters to me, but which are only intended for Him (sic), rest assured that he has the common sense to view them in their proper light and will consider you a mere sycophant.' This letter was in turn copied to Isaac and is in his papers. It appears that Isaac finally arbitrated on this dispute in April.

Crothers' wife, Agnes, Isaac's sister died in childbirth in August 1873 leaving him with the newborn child and his two other daughters to care for. Albert Holden Illingworth, the second son of Henry Illingworth and Mary Holden, married Isaac Holden Crothers' daughter, Annie Elizabeth in 1895. Albert went on to become the chairman of Isaac Holden et Fils, a Liberal MP and then Baron Illingworth. He served under David Lloyd George as Post Master General during the First World War.

The two nephews continued their rivalry and in December 1878 Isaac wrote to warn them, 'I must have each concern working at the top of its capital and will use all the means for doing so without friction – else we can't go on'. In 1880 matters finally came to a head when Jonathan threatened to finally leave Isaac Holden et Fils and set up in business on his own. Isaac went to see Jonathan in the January, but concluded a break with him was inevitable. Jonathan resigned and set up a rival business in Reims, which became known as the 'Nouvel Anglais'. Isaac Crothers became the general manager of both the Isaac Holden et Fils Croix and Reims factories known as the 'Vieux Anglais'; the Reims factory being managed by Lewthwaite who was in turn succeeded by his sons, John and

Robert. [John Lewthwaite was the manager when his deputy, John Hodgson and five members of staff – Leon Carvenant, Albert Foster, Tom Whitaker, Rayner Smith and Marcel Thiebaut - stayed in the factory under shellfire during the bombardment of Reims in the First World War and successfully removed several hundred thousand kilos of tops and raw wool.]

Visiting Reims in April Isaac reported to Sarah that Jonathon had not taken his son, John Edward, into the new business because he had become addicted to gambling and had lost £14,000 in a single night in Paris. Isaac Crothers told him that Jonathan had paid off John's gambling bills of £50,000 (more than £4 million in today's terms) but that when further bills had come to light Jonathan had packed him off to Algiers.

On July 1 1884 Isaac wrote from Reims, 'We spent yesterday visiting several of our customers and we found Jonathan is condemned by them… We take possession (of the factory) today and are putting the new men into their places'.

Jonathan's 'Nouvel Anglais' factory at 61 Boulevard Dauphinot prospered. On the occasion of Queen Victoria's Jubilee in 1887 he founded an elegant free library in Reims. Learning about this Angus Holden disingenuously suggested to Isaac, 'This is a crafty bid for popularity – worthy of its author… would it not be politic on our part to present say 50,000 francs to the municipality of Roubaix and 50,000 to Reims'.

Jonathan had shown himself to be man of considerable courage who took great risks to look after the interest of his workers in the Franco-Prussian war. Jonathan Holden was made a Knight of the Legion of Honor, the highest decoration in France. There is still to this day a Rue Jonathan Holden named after him in Reims.

Mary Susannah Sugden, Sarah Sugden's niece, who had married Jonathan Holden's son, John Edward, died at the age of 32. Shortly afterwards John Edward came to Bradford and asked his Aunt Sarah if he could visit Isaac, but Isaac churlishly declined to do so. John Edward wrote a bitter letter of reproach, 'For the last 9 years, for reasons of your own, you have chosen to ignore me and mine.' Reminding Isaac that his father had been Isaac's business partner for 12 years, he suggested 'you have chosen to boycott him through jealousy'. John Edward died two years later.

When Jonathan Holden's first wife, Tamar Gill, died in 1892 he married Sarah Ellen Sugden. Jonathan died and was buried in Reims in 1906. His body was eventually disinterred and reburied in the family plot at the Undercliffe cemetery alongside his children and Isaac and Sarah Holden. According to the cemetery guidebook the mausoleum that stands over the Holden Family graves was erected in memory of 'Jonathan Holden of Reims and Algiers'.

12. The Phoenix Park murders and a return to parliament

In October 1878, Alfred Illingworth began to seek a rapprochement with W.E. Forster and to bring to an end their hostilities over the Education Act in return for Forster's pledge to support the disestablishment of the Church in Scotland. This paved the way for their joint nomination as the two Liberal candidates for Bradford in the next election. Henry Ripley, the former Liberal MP, was nominated as the Conservative candidate. Illingworth's association with Forster worked in his favour as he had become to be seen as anti-trade union because of his intransigent stance on recent strikes. At the general election in April 1880 Alfred Illingworth was elected as the member for Bradford alongside W.E. Forster, who topped the poll and now became the Chief Secretary for Ireland.

Irish Home Rule

Irish Home Rule and the Reform Bill were to dominate the new administration. The situation in Ireland was dire with failed harvests and economic depression. Tenant farmers anger was directed to intransigent landlords who failed to reduce rents in these hardened times. A National Land League, formed in Ireland in October 1879, organised a boycott of the rising number of landlords and farmers who took over farms or paid rent once a farmer had been evicted.

W. E. Forster introduced the Irish Land Bill in 1881 providing tenants with new rights, 'the three Fs' of Fair Rent, Fixity of tenure and Free sale (of tenant right). The Bill had the effect of limiting the absolute power of the Irish landlords. Isaac Holden chaired a heated public meeting in Bradford, which had a significant Irish population, at which Forster spoke on the Irish Land Bill on May 11th 1881. The Chief Constable had warned Forster beforehand that he was at risk of being shot. Interestingly from Isaac's point of view Forster and Illingworth also met the local Chamber of Commerce the following day to discuss trade negotiations with France over higher tariffs.

The atmosphere in the House of Commons when the Bill was passed was equally heated, because the recent Protection (or Coercion) Act - giving the authorities special powers of arrest and detention without trial - provoked the Irish leader, Charles Stewart Parnell, to adopt obstructive tactics to delay parliamentary business. After a Cabinet meeting and instruction on October 12th Parnell was imprisoned under the Protection Act in Dublin, because of his outspoken support for increasingly violent anti-English protest in Ireland by the members of the Land League. He was not released until the following April.

The Radical Liberal, Joseph Chamberlain, brokered an agreement with Parnell, using the MP for County Clare, Captain O'Shea, as an intermediary, to secure his release. O'Shea's wife, Kitty, was Parnell's mistress. In Cabinet Forster strongly opposed his release and subsequently resigned as Chief Secretary for Ireland. When Forster together with Illingworth subsequently attended a constituency meeting in Bradford on December 7th Illingworth praised his handling of the crisis, "not a word which has fallen from him should in the slightest degree lessen your regard for him."

Lord Frederick Cavendish, a large Irish landowner, replaced Forster as Chief Secretary. Three days after Parnell's release members of the Invicibles, a radical splinter group of the Irish Republican Brotherhood, assassinated Cavendish and his permanent secretary Thomas Burke on May 6th 1882 whilst walking in Dublin's Phoenix Park.

The assassination of Lord Frederick Cavendish led to a by-election for which Isaac Holden (now aged 75) was quickly selected as the Liberal candidate for the Northern Division of the West Riding of Yorkshire. Speaking at an election rally at Todmorden reported in the Leeds Mercury on May 15th, Isaac spoke in favour of further Irish land reforms, against the policy of coercion and in favour of 'justice and conciliation'. His Tory opponent spoke at a rally in Keighley at which Tories paraded with mock placards in Liberal orange proclaiming, 'Vote for Holden and the Land League'. At the declaration of the poll Isaac comfortably won the seat with 9,802 votes against 7,805. Isaac addressed a crowd of several thousand outside the Keighley Liberal Club and his own 'brilliantly illuminated' grounds were thrown open to the public in celebration.

Lady Cavendish sent Isaac a warm telegram of congratulations, 'The great majority has cheered me and made me thankful'. On the day before the ringleader was hanged Lady Cavendish had sent him the small gold crucifix she had long worn, as a token of her forgiveness. Lady Cavendish, who was Catherine Gladstone's niece, told Gladstone that she could bear the loss of her beloved husband "if his death were to work good to his fellow-men." She, like Isaac, remained a firm supporter of Home Rule for Ireland.

Just three weeks after the assassination of Cavendish on May 23rd Isaac was sworn in as the new Member for the West Riding. 'As soon as I had taken the oath Mr. Gladstone, Mr. Bright and others of the Ministers gave me a hearty shake of the hand and welcomed me most cordially.'

The typical parliamentary day started at 4.30, generally adjourning for dinner at 7.30, and then continuing with debates until 1.30 or even 2.30 am. In spite of his advanced years, Isaac took his duties in the Commons seriously during this session of parliament. During long sittings in the House Isaac lent his support to Gladstone's Arrears Bill, which had the effect of cancelling the rent arrears of Irish tenants occupying land worth less than £30 per year. One of ten Wesleyan members Isaac saw it as their duty to give, 'cordial support to the "Grand Old Man". Isaac observed, 'When I see Mr. Gladstone always at his weary work sitting by the Table and listening to idle and often offensive speeches, I really don't allow myself to feel tired, so that I generally stay to the last and wish to continue my work till we get the business finished.' Often this would be to 2 am or later when he would take a tumbler of hot whisky on returning to his lodgings at Queen Anne's Mansions.

Nevertheless Sarah continued to chide him for not being at home more but his response was to refer to the 'sense of duty (which) supports me in being deprived of these dear pleasures.' Isaac wrote to Sarah on almost a daily basis whenever he was sitting in the Commons. They were generally short missives but occasionally quite affectionate in nature: 'I only wish I could go for the air and walks (at Oakworth) but also that I might have you in my arms every night. That is very sweet to me and does me good.'

Gladstone had first been called the Grand Old Man (GOM) by Henry Labouchere when speaking at a by-election in Northampton in support of Charles Bradlaugh, an atheist, who had been forced to fight a successful by-election in 1881 after attempting to affirm rather than take the religiously-based Oath of Allegiance on entering parliament the year before. The Bradlaugh saga took up a great deal of parliamentary time with no less than two select committees. After a long battle Bradlaugh, who became popular with his parliamentary colleagues, eventually forced a change in the law with the passing of the Affirmation Bill by a Tory government in 1888.

Despite their religious differences Isaac befriended Bradlaugh. They shared an equally passionate interest in promoting the channel tunnel, a hot topic of debate in the 1870s and 1880s. [In 1861 Isaac had bought £4,000 worth of shares in the Sub Marine Telegraph Company.] The first serious attempt to build a tunnel came with an Act of Parliament in 1875 authorising the Channel Tunnel Company Ltd to start preliminary trials. Following a panic in 1883, led by those fearing it would lead to a French invasion, tunnelling stopped. In 1887 Charles Bradlaugh wrote a book, *The Channel tunnel: ought the democracy to oppose or support it?*

After Bradlaugh died the *Freethinker* on October 22nd 1893 contained an article by Mr. George Standring giving an account of a Sunday service he attended at the Wesley Chapel in the City-road. The preacher on that occasion was the Rev. Allen Rees, and the theme of his discourse was "The Death of the *National Reformer*". Standring recorded the preacher as saying:

> 'Indeed, there was reason to believe that Charles Bradlaugh had himself materially modified his views before his death, that his Atheism became weaker as he grew older. Sir Isaac Holden had told him (Mr. Rees) that Mr. Bradlaugh had often spoken to him privately in the House of Commons upon religious matters, and had admitted that the conversion of his brother (Bradlaugh's) had profoundly impressed him. Mr. Bradlaugh had often

said to Sir Isaac Holden that he often wished he were half as good a man as his brother'.

Bradlaugh's daughter, Mrs Bonner, wrote asking him whether he 'really did tell this to the Rev. Allen Rees', but Isaac failed to reply. Mrs Bonner evidently remarked on 'the obviously loose reminiscences of Sir Isaac Holden', which Mr. Rees had 'materially altered', and denied the possibility of any such conversation between Sir Isaac Holden and her father.

Vaccination

According to his later obituaries the two pet subjects on which Isaac, who was normally silent in the chamber of the House of Commons, could be relied on to ask a question about were the building of the channel tunnel and the campaign against compulsory vaccination for small pox.

The Vaccination Act of 1853 ordered mandatory vaccination against small pox for infants up to three months old, and the Act of 1867 extended this age requirement to fourteen years, adding penalties for vaccine refusal. The Anti-Compulsory Vaccination League was founded in 1867 in response to the new law. Isaac's constituency of Keighley was at the centre of the controversy when in 1875 the local board of guardians dropped all parental prosecutions and sacked their vaccination officer. Some members of the board of guardians were briefly imprisoned in York Castle.

The friend even of bitter Tories

When he turned 80 in 1888 the political columnist of *The Star* wrote a pen portrait of Isaac describing him as:

'One of the smallest men in the House of Commons; and he is slight and thin. A peculiar feature of Mr. Holden is the brilliance of his eyes.

Mr. Holden is one of the most devoted frequenters of the smoke room in the House of Commons. And he doesn't smoke the mildest cigarette; a good long cigar is what he likes, though he keeps shorter and milder cigars for the use of less robust friends.

He never speaks in the House of Commons but he is a brilliant conversationalist. In politics he is a thorough going Radical. Ireland has no truer friend. There is no sitting too long or too late for him if there is a division in which a vote can be given for Ireland. Though staunch in his own creed, the gentle and calm tolerance of his nature fit him as the friend even of bitter Tories. To them and everybody he is willing to discourse on his favourite topics: the folly of overeating, the necessity for improved knowledge of physiology, and the daily walk as the best of all preservatives of health'.

London was on occasion covered in smog in the winter months, which Isaac complained aggravated his bronchitis. He walked on most days from his rooms at Queen Anne's mansions in Petty France to the Reform Club on the south side of Pall Mall. Liberal members of the two Houses of Parliament founded the Reform Club designed by Sir Charles Barry in 1836. On inclement days he would take his daily walk in the Reform's great hall with friends including John Bright. Dining at the Reform with its renowned cuisine, Isaac would then retire to the smoking room before returning to parliament for the evening session.

The gregarious Isaac befriended MPs on both sides of the House and would visit them at their own homes. One visit to Mr Palmer, the Liberal Member for Reading, "Quaker (who) spoke of their liberality to Methodists", resulted in a visit to their "wonderful Biscuit Manufactory" (Huntley & Palmers). He always accepted invitations to soirees and more formal events, such as the Speakers levee when he instructed Sarah to 'send me my court dress and sword and also the feather for my cocked hat'.

Isaac befriended Mrs Gladstone who involved Isaac in her good causes; he visited a Convalescent House with her and Mr Gladstone in 1884. He wrote to her in curiously intimate terms on the occasion of her 75th birthday saying he wished to contribute to Mr. Gladstone's health by sending a few bottles of a solution of oil which he used following his morning bath taken 'at 80 degrees temperature in which I use a soap lather to cleanse the skin thoroughly with friction in which I am assisted by a valet who employs it in his whole force for some twenty minutes. I then moisten the entire surface of the body inclusive of the head and face with the solution which I now send.' He would instruct Sarah to send flowers to No. 10 Downing Street from the hot houses at Oakworth.

His friendship with Mrs Gladstone resulted in her presenting his daughters, Mary and Margaret, at Queen Victoria's Court in May 1888. Margaret wrote to her father to describe how, 'The beautiful diamonds you gave us were all duly worn and were quite worth the occasion.'

Mary was a dedicated follower of fashion; this can be seen both in her diaries and through the beautiful clothes that have survived and are now exhibited at Leeds City Museum. She bought a number of dresses from the famous designer Charles Frederick Worth. Mary recounted to her granddaughter, Elsie, how 'fittings were of dubious delight, as Monsieur Worth was of the habit of taking a cup of warm fresh blood straight from the local abattoir at 11 am'.

The Olden and the Young un

Gladstone's Government was defeated on the Budget in June 1885. Isaac wrote ruefully home on June 9th, 'In consequence of the resignation of the Government I shall come down tomorrow. It was owing to the carelessness and absence of many Liberal members that the Government was defeated'.

In the ensuing general election the 79-year-old Isaac stood successfully for the newly created Keighley division. His son, Angus, was elected for East Bradford and his son-in-law, Alfred, for West Bradford. Angus had focussed in his campaign on the radical Nonconformist causes of church disestablishment and, interestingly, the reconstitution of the House of Lords: 'The hereditary principle is out of harmony with the spirit of the age.'

Isaac received a letter of congratulation from Annie Lucy, wife of Sir Henry Lucy the parliamentary sketch-writer whose nom-de-plume in Punch was "Toby, M.P.": 'Mr. Lucy says there will be no difficulty in distinguishing between you two in the House of Commons, you will of course be known as the Olden and the Young un.' Angus, who had already served four terms as Mayor of Bradford, seems to have stuck closely with Isaac in his early days in the House of Commons. He was to lose his seat in the 1886 election and did not return to parliament until he was elected as a Liberal for the Buckrose Division of the East Riding in 1892.

Parnell's Home Rulers gained 86 seats in the House of Commons denying the Liberals an overall majority. However on January 26th 1886 the Liberals were able to vote down the Tories on the Queen's speech and Gladstone formed his third administration committed to Home Rule with the support of Parnell. The Radical leaders Chamberlain and Bright, and the Whig, Lord Hartington, did not share Gladstone's commitment to Home Rule but Isaac and other more prominent northern Radicals, including John Morley and Alfred Illingworth, did so. Much to Chamberlain's chagrin Morley became Gladstone's Irish Secretary. Alfred Illingworth, who famously described Chamberlain as a "traitor", was to play a prominent role in persuading other Nonconformists to support Home Rule.

Isaac took part in a meeting of 50 Liberal Home Rule supporters chaired by Illingworth in the House of Commons on May 11th 1886 and agreed to go on a committee to organise support for the second reading of the Home Rule Bill. However Chamberlain effectively mobilised the Liberal opposition to the Bill at a meeting on May 31st. John Bright, who did not attend the infamous meeting, wrote a letter to Chamberlain announcing his decision to vote against the second reading. The Bill was defeated in a House of Commons vote on June 7th, when 93 Liberals including Chamberlain and Bright voted against the Government forcing Gladstone to call a general election in which the Liberals were resoundingly defeated. The Liberal Party was now split with Gladstonian supporters of Home Rule being put up against those opposing it, the Liberal Unionists, in many constituencies. Standing as a Gladstonian Liberal candidate Isaac was returned unopposed for Keighley and Alfred Illingworth won in West Bradford, but Angus Holden lost his seat in East Bradford.

Gladstone's parliamentary defeat over Home Rule had split the Liberal party but Isaac remained loyal to him and the Irish cause. Isaac also felt it his duty to support the Irish leader Charles Parnell.

157

On August 25th 1886 he told Sarah he had just been 'into the House to hear Parnell's very able speech... delivered in his usual calm but effective style' and again on February 21st 1887, 'I think it would have been rum if I had not come up to support Parnell.' Together with a handful of Radicals he voted for Parnell's Irish Land Bill in 1888.

As a Gladstonian Liberal described in the Methodist Times as a 'Monomaniacal Gladstonian', Isaac paid for a bust of Gladstone by John Adams Acton at the recently completed National Liberal Club. On July 27th 1889 he attended a lavish celebration of Gladstone's Golden Wedding at the Reform Club.

13. For fear of saying hard things

Isaac maintained a strong interest and oversight of his business affairs and paid regular visits to his factories in France. After 1886 profits had begun to fall dramatically as costs rose in the Reims factory. At his behest in 1888 Angus Holden and Henry Illingworth set about restructuring the business and making large-scale economies. Proposing to leave 'the especial men' for later consideration, Isaac urged them to weed out 'the non-especial men'. Angus and Henry recommended changes at Reims, which brought about a saving of 100,000 francs (around £4,000) in the wages bill. Similar measures were taken after their visit to Croix.

After he made a follow up visit to Croix in November 1888, Isaac wrote a letter to one of the 'especial men' the mechanic, John Metcalfe, demanding to know what improvements they had originated and if there was any justification for the 'unusually large salaries' he and his son, Tom, were paid. John Metcalfe responded by saying that after 39 years of faithful service he never expected to have to answer such an 'astonishing letter'. He went on to explain in detail the improvements to the combing process he and his son had implemented with one fixed idea, 'that of keeping the place at the top of the tree'. Metcalfe went on to suggest that 'if a cold has been cast over the place' it had been brought on by, 'the thousands and tens of thousands that have been swallowed up by people who never did any good to the place and who never appeared to have any idea but one and that was to draw all they could out of the place

159

without turning a finger to help the work'. He stopped there 'for fear of saying hard things'.

Reminding Metcalfe, 'It is my duty to know the full merits of anyone on your position and acknowledge and reward them accordingly', Isaac responded by going on to praise his good management. However a month later he took issue with Metcalfe's claims to innovation and showed his own hubris, 'I have a distinct recollection of having originated all the improvements you name.' The retention of this correspondence may suggest that Isaac may have subsequently reflected on the role his sons were playing in the enterprise and their enormous drawings from it.

Lister's Hubris: "It was I that did it and I alone."

In February 1879, the London Society Illustrated Magazine published an extended profile of Isaac Holden in a series written by James Burnley entitled 'Fortunes made in Business'. Burnley wrote to Isaac in September 1886 proposing to update his profile in a new book, which was also to include profiles of Sir William Armstrong, Sir James Kitson, Sir Andrew Fairburn and Lister. Burnley asked Isaac for £16 to meet the cost of a new portrait to illustrate the article.

His former partner had written to Burnley taking issue with Isaac's claims over the Square Motion comb in the earlier profile. Burnley shared the drafts with each of them. When Lister amended his draft profile to insert reference to an earlier 'arbitration' submitted by Lister to Richard Webster QC, the then Attorney General, and Mr. Aston, who apparently decided, 'the claim put forward by Mr. Holden of having suggested the Square Motion was not borne out by the facts contained in his letter written at that time, December 25th 1852', Burnley wrote to Isaac telling him he had declined to accept this amendment.

Lister's response was to write directly to Isaac (in the form of a printed letter or pamphlet) offering to go to arbitration again and suggesting whichever party lost should pay £10,000 to the Hospital for Sick Children. Lister went on to say that Jonathan Holden had told him in France that Isaac had nothing to do with inventing any combing whatsoever. Burnley also received a visit from Jonathan and wrote to Isaac on December 22nd saying, 'I have had a sort of mist thrown over me out of which I should have been glad of your guidance.'

Somewhat surprisingly Lister then wrote to Burnley on January 15th 1887 conceding:

> *'The "Nip" machine came so close upon the heels of the Square Motion that it had scarcely passed the experimental stage before it was superseded. For France we could not use the Nip on account of Heilman's patent – and so we had no choice but to work it – and in that way it may be said to have become Mr. Holden's child but in no other sense'.*

Nevertheless the acrimonious correspondence continued and sometime between January and March 1887 the Attorney General and Mr Aston gave what was evidently a legal opinion, which Isaac told Burnley, 'does not amount to much'. In July Lister resorted to threatening Burnley with legal action if he were to publish Isaac's claims.

On July 25th 1887 Burnley wrote to Isaac announcing he was planning another new book, 'The History of Wool and Wool-Combing', which Isaac subsequently offered to sponsor. In the preface to

161

'The History of Wool And Wool-Combing', which was first published in a handsomely bound edition in 1889, Burnley was careful both to thank Isaac Holden 'for permission to refer to his private, Retrospective Notes on Woolcombing'; to Lister 'for his kindness in affording me information on many points'; and 'to Mr. Jonathan Holden for giving me particulars of special interest and moment'.

'As for the Square Motion, as originally patented,' Burnley wrote in 'The History of Woolcombing', 'it was almost incapable of combing wool; it took years of effort and the co-operation of many practical minds to bring it to perfection.'

At the end of 1888 Donnisthorpe's son became mired in the dispute with Lister who wrote to him denying his father's role in the early development of the Square Motion. In a subsequent letter to Donnisthorpe's son, Lister claimed in response 'to the important question: "Who made the combing of fine wool, practical by machinery; and who made it a great commercial success *"IT WAS I THAT DID AND I ALONE."'*

After 'The History of Wool And Wool-Combing' was published in 1889 Burnley, who had praised Isaac's inventiveness, came under pressure from Lister 'who never ceased to contend that I had done him less than justice'. In 1904, he was compelled to withdraw what Lister had seen as 'calumniating statements' made in the book. Lister then put Burnley's letter of withdrawal in the opening pages of his own book, 'Lord Masham's Inventions written by himself', published in 1905, in which he describes his own invention of the Square Motion comb.

Burnley's letter of withdrawal referred to Lister's patent taken out in 1846. 'I find that such Patent contains the first patented embodiment of the principle of the "Square Motion" invention',

Burnley wrote, 'and that having been published before you became acquainted with Mr. Isaac Holden, the statement in my book on the History of Wool And Wool-Combing viz., that "the first patent in which the Square Motion principle was brought forward was dated the 19th of October 1848," is necessarily incorrect'. However, Lister had first become acquainted with Isaac in 1845, when they first discussed taking out a carding patent, so Lister's claim that "*IT WAS I THAT DID AND I ALONE*" remains questionable. In 1905, Lister was still claiming to be the inventor but conceded, 'Although there can be no doubt that I was the inventor, still it was a worthless machine until it was improved by the Holdens.'

A Speculative Son: Railways and a Glaciarium

Edward Holden was determined to prove his worth to his father by entering into increasingly risky speculative ventures on his own behalf. He had been drawn into large-scale investment in the West Lancashire Railway (WLR), which aimed to connect his hometown of Southport with Preston and Blackburn to the north and Liverpool to the south. Work began on the section from Southport to Preston in 1873 but was promptly halted due to lack of capital. In 1876 Edward joined the WLR Board and his injection of capital enabled an initial section of line to be opened. Edward was repeatedly called upon to increase his investment as expensive engineering work was required, so that by January 1888 his stock holding in the West Lancashire Railway had reached a staggering £292,245 (or £26,700,000 in today's terms), much of which was advanced in cash for engineering work. By this stage the WLR and its sister company, the Southport and Preston Junction Railway, were in receivership to Edward.

Matters came to a head in August 1888 when he wrote to his father admitting: 'The West Lancashire Railway is not doing as well as we would like on account on the smallpox epidemic at Preston ... I assure you dear Father it is a very trying time and it is only hope that keeps me up. Had it not been for you I should have lost all.' On September 24th Edward wrote to his father thanking him for a further cash injection of £4,000.

The Only Real Ice Skating & Curling Hall in the World

Edward also invested in the Southport Glaciarium & Ice Manufacturing Company of which he was the Chairman and main stakeholder. The rink, built at a cost of £30,000 (or £2.5 million in today's terms), was opened in 1879 and advertised as: '*The Only Real Ice Skating & Curling Hall in the World: Atmosphere always Dry, Pure and Clear.*' The reference to 'dry, pure and clear' atmosphere was because the earliest rinks had used a noxious ice substitute of hog's lard and a mixture of salts to provide year-round 'ice' skating. In 1876 John Gamgee had opened the world's first mechanically frozen ice rink, the London Glaciarium. The Gamgee refrigeration process, which was used at Southport, was expensive as the rink was based on a concrete surface, with layers of earth, cow hair and timber planks overlaid with oval copper pipes carrying a solution of glycerine with ether, nitrogen peroxide and water. These pipes were covered by water and the solution was pumped through, freezing the water into ice. The system had many problems and Edward poured capital in to get it working properly.

The great event at the Glaciarium was a bi-annual curling tournament for the Holden Challenge Shield, value 30 guineas, presented by Edward himself. In April 1889 the Glaciarium closed its doors with a loss of £25,000 (£2.2 million in today's terms) the burden of which was mainly borne by Edward. The Scot, Mr M'Inroy, wrote a lament for its closure:

> *Alas on Southport ice no more*
> *Shall sound again the curlers roar*
> *The song of 'Nightingale' is hushed,*
> *And Holden's hopes for ever crushed.*

Edward had been financing his speculations by drawing money from the family firm. In addition to the railway and Glaciarium he had also bought a local farm and the temperance 'Coffee Palace' in Shipley which was opened to entice the working classes away from drink (the Queens Palace theatre was later built on the site). Put under pressure from Angus to put a stop to Edward's heavy drawings, in March 1889 Isaac wrote to Edward remonstrating with him. 'I am overwhelmed with grief', Edward responded, 'I will not run away from it whatever happens'. He went on to propose selling the cattle in the farm to help meet his bills.

After Angus had met Edward on July 12th 1889 to go through his finances with him, he wrote to Isaac telling him that Edward estimated his income for the year ahead to be £5,080 (£461,000 in today's terms) 'so it appears he has ample income for his requirements without drawing from the business.' The same day Isaac handed over another cheque to Edward for £4,362 (£396,000 in today's terms) to help him meet his immediate debts.

Isaac's underwriting of Edward's investment in the West Lancashire Railway helped to stop the rot and he also intervened to change the management of the company. By September 1889 Edward was able to write more optimistically to his father, 'The public are having confidence in us. Our shares cannot be had, no one will part with what they hold.'

Isaac had speculated in railway shares himself during the railway bubble of 1845. Later he was the Chairman of the Keighley and Worth Valley Railway cutting the railway's first sod on Shrove Tuesday, February 9th 1864 and investing more than £16,000 in it, partly in order to secure a station at Oakworth (since made famous by the film, The Railway Children, released in 1970). In 1884 he had also bought several thousand pounds of railway stock in conjunction with Miss Pickles.

Angus was still writing to Isaac in 1894 asking that Edward's affairs and the business partnership be put on 'satisfactory basis before the end of the year'. However Angus also lived an extravagant lifestyle. In 1889 he rented a 6-bedroom house in Paris for six months in the fashionable Avenue Henri Martin complete with a valet, cook and a chambermaid, so that he could attend the Paris Exhibition. [Winnaretta Singer, heiresses of the sewing machine magnate, built her fashionable house and salon in this street.] In 1890 Angus purchased Nun Appleton Hall, a 17th Century country house and estate, originally the seat of the Fairfax family, thus becoming one of several members of Bradford's Millocracy who moved into the "county set". Eight years before Lister had bought the castle and large country estate at Swinton Park in the Yorkshire Dales.

14. Health & Longevity, a Baronetcy and a Strike

The preservation of his personal and business reputation was clearly a major reason behind Isaac's intervention to bail out Edward. Largely because of his wealth and longevity he was being feted in the press. The columnist for the *New York Tribune* wrote on January 24th 1889:

> 'The richest man, probably, in the British House of Commons, is Mr. Isaac Holden ... The average sum he receives every year is something like $1,000,000. Like most millionaires, the habits of Mr. Holden are as simple as a clerk with thirty shillings a week'.

If I get heavier then I cut off the supplies

His reputation for living a healthy lifestyle was echoed in an article by the London correspondent of the *Manchester Guardian*:

> 'Mr Holden attributes his extraordinary vigour and unbroken health at 82 years to a persistent diet of fruit. For many years past he has made it a rule to eat two meals of fruit every day, and his third meal is largely composed of vegetables'.

Isaac believed that by following a regime of a strict diet and exercise he could live to be 120. In his 86th year he gave an extended interview at Oakworth to the *Bradford Observer* on the subject of 'Health and Longevity', subsequently published as a booklet. Taking the interviewer into his library, Isaac showed him his collections of books on physiology. From his reading and experimentation he told him he had deduced that flesh meat is only needed in small quantities to renew muscle waste and only if you take regular exercise. Hence he took "two hours exercise in the open air every forenoon" and in his early career had made it a condition of his tenure at Cullingworth mills that he had a two-hour break for exercise. He also told the interviewer that the air in the room in which they were sitting at Oakworth had changed three times since the beginning of their interview thanks to the ventilation system he had installed, "and you will always find the thermometer in this room all the year round at about 62 or 63 degrees."

Eating sparingly and living largely on fruit he aimed to keep his weight at 8 stones and 6 pounds, 'If I get heavier then I cut off the supplies". A follower of Buchan's Domestic Medicine (1769), Isaac also declared himself in favour of daily "tubbing" in cold or tepid water - Buchan had advocated regular bathing as a germ inhibitor - and of the Turkish baths he took regularly at Oakworth and in London.

Rewards exist for right actions

Sarah Holden died on May 3rd 1890. She had been married to Isaac for 40 years. Her funeral service was held at Oakworth Wesleyan chapel and she was buried at the Undercliffe cemetery in Bradford. Isaac's only known reference to her death was in a somewhat cryptic comment he made in an interview with Emily Crawford (for a character sketch published in the 'Review of Reviews'):

"Had she only followed strictly my dietetic rules, she would still be alive." Sarah left £487 in her Will.

Offered a Baronetcy by Gladstone in 1884 Isaac declined because Sarah was opposed to his accepting it. He was created a Baronet after her death in 1893, the year of the Queen's Jubilee, taking as his motto on the family crest, *'Rewards exist for right actions'*. A letter from the Home Department advised him, 'for obtaining Letters Patent under the Great Seal conferring upon you the Dignity of a Baronetcy of the United Kingdom. I have to request you will at your earliest convenience forward a cheque for £309… to enable the Secretary of State to defray the (necessary) expenses.'

Samuel Lister became a peer two years earlier and took the title Lord Masham. An article in *The Yorkshireman* amusingly parodied the two appointments in the form of a three Act play in blank verse:

Act One opens with S.C.L. (Samuel Cunliffe Lister) writing a letter to the press:

"he ne'er invented e'en a single screw," –

Though much he has draw mine – "twas I alone

This same square motion gave unto the world".

Act Three has a character saying to S.C.L.:

"Square motion did you say! That brings to mind

A baronetcy Holden once declined."

To which S.C.L. responds:

"Take Holden's leavings!

No I never will!

As Lord Square Motion then,

Or Lister still."

The Manningham Mills Strike and the 1892 West Bradford Election

Since selling his share in the French concerns to Isaac, Lister's business had prospered. After his first factory was burnt down in 1871 he built the magnificent Italianate Manningham Mills complete with a 255 ft. campanile chimneystack. Employing 11,000 men, women and children it was the largest silk factory in the world and also produced worsted and velvet cloth. By 1889 exports made up two-thirds of its sales.

Lister claimed to have a million pounds invested in Manningham, a million in tea in India and a million in coal; he owned a colliery near Pontefract providing Manningham Mills with 50,000 tons of coal a year. In 1883 he bought the 23,000 acres Swinton Park estate at Masham in Wensleydale for £400,000 (or £33 million in today's terms) and four years later acquired the adjoining estate on which Jervaulx Abbey stands.

An avowed protectionist Lister was the President of the National Fare Trade League, formed in 1881 to campaign for protectionism, and one of its major subscribers. He had read a lecture entitled, England's Folly, at the Silk Section of the Jubilee Exhibition in Manchester on October 21st 1887 in which he blamed the current state of the silk trade on 'the free importation of foreign goods, and that Free Trade is the cause of all our loss and trouble.' Taking John Bright to task for claiming that 'Free Trade has raised the working men's wages he used the example of the period of the Franco-Prussian War (1870-74), 'when our markets were practically protected from invasion' as providing 'the years of our greatest prosperity'. Arguing that the silk trade was being irreparably damaged by free foreign imports he went on to propose taxing foreign silks and to attack 'the blindness of the working classes' in supporting as system of Free Trade. With regard to the woollen industry, he asked the rhetorical question, 'Is it for the national advantage and general prosperity because French goods can be imported 5 per cent cheaper?'

Three years after giving this lecture Lister's silk exports to the USA were very badly affected by the introduction of the McKinley tariffs in 1890, which increased average duties across all imports to the USA by 49.5 per cent. Less than a month after the passing of the McKinley tariffs Lister, 'American Sam', had two representatives looking at potential sites in Philadelphia to relocate his factories to America.

At home his response was to demand that his silk plushers accept wage reductions to their already low wages of between 20 to 35 per cent. A strike/lockout began shortly before Christmas 1890; initially around a thousand workers were involved, but the strike soon spread to other parts of the mill as wages were reduced.

Threatening to close down the mill and move production Lister wrote to the *Bradford Observer* on Boxing Day disparaging his workforce:

> *'That they have earned in the past not only good wages but very good wages, is certain, or the Manningham ladies, the "plushers", as they are called could not dress in the way they do. Silks and flounces, hats and feathers, no lady in the town can be finer. No one likes better to see them comfortably and befittingly dressed than I do; but there is reason in all things. But what is the moral of all*

this? What I never cease to preach and teach - utter want of thrift. The women spend their money on dress and the men in drink; so the begging box goes round - it matters not what their wages are'.

By March the number of strikers totalled over 4,000 and production was brought to a standstill. On March 26th, 20,000 people attended a procession through Bradford. Although the local Watch Committee refused permission for an open air meeting next to St Georges Hall on Sunday April 12th thousands still gathered to listen to speakers such as Ben Tillett, who had successfully led the London Dock Strike two years earlier. The next day the Mayor, Mr E. W. Hammond, read the Riot Act and 106 soldiers of the Durham Light Infantry, 'paraded the streets with bayonets drawn and charged the people in various directions…As a result of the evening's violence, many were injured and 10 men were arrested'. After 19 weeks the workers were forced back to work.

Precipitated by the Manningham Mills strike, the politics of Bradford became more volatile with Ben Tillett standing as an independent labour candidate against Alfred Illingworth in Bradford West in the 1892 general election. Tillett's candidature was motivated by his anger with the official Liberals in the town, including Illingworth, who had joined hands with the Tories to bring troops in to quell the Manningham strike. Tillett was also excoriating in challenging Illingworth's attitude to child labour and his opposition to the eight-hour day. As Jonathan Schneer has shown in his biography of Ben Tillett, alarmed by the prospect of his candidature, Liberal Party representatives offered him an unopposed contest if he stood against the Conservatives in Bradford East and a hundred pounds towards his expenses. Naturally Tillett dismissed this crude manoeuvre out of hand.

Liberal trade unionists in the wool trades came out in support of Alfred Illingworth. These included the Machine Woolcombers Society whose secretary, Samuel Shaftoe, was an active member of the Bradford Liberal Association. Schneer speculates that they may well have been influenced by Illingworth's position as a dominant employer in Bradford and by their own 'hard-won' position in the Liberal Party Association. It cannot, however, have been out of any great love for the employers. Samuel Shaftoe later gave a graphic account of working conditions and employment in the woollen industry in an interview in The Star on January 13th 1898 with night combers earning 17 to 24 shillings a week for a 63 hour week in temperatures of 96 to 100 degrees Farenheit.

Fenner Brockway described Tillett with his trademark broad rimmed black hat and loose black coat as having 'a magnetic personality' and 'the idealism of an evangelist'. A Congregationalist, who preached in labour churches, Tillett used biblical references in his speeches. Prominent trade union and labour leaders spoke for him during the campaign, including his fellow leader of the Dockers' Union, Tom Mann, and the Fabian Socialist, Sidney Webb. At a meeting convened at the Mechanics Institute on June 13th 1892 to endorse Illingworth's candidature, local Labour leader Fred Jowett made an impassioned speech and moved a resolution describing Tillett as 'at least as good a Nonconformist as Mr. Alfred Illingworth'. Jowett warned the meeting: "If you persist in opposing the Labour Movement there will be more reason than ever to complain of the absence of working men from your chapels. We shall establish our own Labour Church." The Bradford Labour Church was formed after this incident. Although the meeting endorsed Illingworth the workingman's voice was now being heard.

Sidney Webb in his review of the election was perceptive in describing Illingworth as 'a sturdy, old fashioned individualist'. He was also a capitalist, who could put his own interests first, as he did during the campaign when he argued against Tillett's proposals for raising the working age of children and reducing the employment hours of working mothers, saying it would be the 'greatest cruelty' to deprive married mothers of the opportunity to work in his factory. Tillett derided such self-interested paternalism, 'The rich capitalist was replacing the old landlord, and he generally took into possession of the land less conscience.'

Illingworth's passionate support for Home Rule, and the endorsement of the Bradford branch of the Irish National League, helped mobilise the sizeable Irish vote in Bradford in his favour. Tillett's intervention in the West Bradford campaign attracted national attention and an incredible turn out of 96 per cent. Illingworth won with 3,306 votes, Flower, the Tory candidate, came second with 3,053 votes and Tillett third with 2,749 votes.

Kier Hardie, the future Labour leader, was elected for West Ham in the 1892 election. Hardie and Tillett both took part in the inaugural meeting of the national Independent Labour Party in Bradford in January 1893. In a lecture looking back at 'Fifty Years in Politics', given at the Westgate Baptist schoolroom in Manningham in 1905, Alfred Illingworth acknowledged the part the Manningham strike had played in the rise of the Socialist movement. He went on to say, 'I do not object to Mr. Ben Tillett, or Mr. Kier Hardie, or any one else looking forward to the millennium when socialism will be the predominant system… and in the meantime they had better work with those who are travelling in this direction – towards the attainable and the possible.'

The problem for Illingworth and the Liberal Party was that they had failed to take account of the increasing demand for collectivist policies to address the needs of the poor revealed by the surveys of Charles Booth and Joseph Rowntree, and the demands of workers for improved wages and working conditions. As Fred Jowett observed, 'Capitalists in Parliament, irrespective of politics were banded together in opposition to legislative measures desired by wage earners'. Their individualistic policies designed to broaden the electorate, address 'dissenters' grievances' and create a 'ladder' of educational opportunities by which enterprising workers could climb up the economic and social system, had failed to address fundamental working class grievances.

15. Death Duties and Isaac's last session in Parliament

The Keighley Labour Union was formed in Isaac's own constituency in 1892. Before the election Isaac became ill with a bronchial condition and went to Algiers for several months to recuperate. Now aged 85 he contemplated not standing again, but was returned to parliament unopposed. Angus Holden also re-joined Isaac in parliament having been elected for the Buckrose Division of the East Riding, which he continued to represent until 1900.

The Gladstonian Liberals now formed a minority government dependent on Irish Nationalist support. Despite the tight electoral results, Gladstone's mission for Home Rule again drove the administration. John Morley, now Gladstone's greatest ally, was his Irish Secretary and William Harcourt, the Chancellor of the Exchequer.

The debate on the unsuccessful Home Rule Bill in 1893 went on for months and with the more than 600 divisions that took place it must have taxed a man of Isaac's age very considerably. "Toby", the parliamentary sketch writer, Lucy, described how on one sultry night on which the Bill was being debated, among the faithful were 'two young fellows', Mr Gladstone in his eighty-fifth year, and Mr. Holden, two years his senior, the latter 'as straight as a dart, his eyes retaining their freshness, his cheek in bloom'. Isaac was at that time the oldest member of the House of Commons with the exception of Charles Pelham Villiers. In March 1895 one of the prominent

Irish nationalists, John Dillon, who had taken part in the negotiations for the 1893 Bill, speaking at a meeting at Keighley Institute personally thanked Isaac for his long-term support for home rule.

Illingworthism: a gospel without sympathy, comradeship, or hope

In 1894 Alfred Illingworth opposed the new government's Miners' Eight Hours Bill. Illingworth argued that he saw great danger in the state interfering with adult labour (as opposed to children and women) and saw no need for exception to be made in the case of the miners, and 'if Parliament so interfered between employers and the employed as to handicap them in their competition with other nations, this would be dangerous too.' Thirty liberals, including Isaac and Angus Holden, voted against the Bill. Illingworth wrote to Sir William Harcourt:

> *'The course taken by Asquith when speaking on the Eight Hours Miners bill filled me with amazement – as did many others. It was expected that he would at least declare on behalf of his colleagues the case for the miners was so exceptional that it would form no precedent for the thousand other industries whose claim for similar legislation might be expected to follow.'*

Although he stood down and did not fight his Bradford seat in the general election in 1895, Illingworth remained a key local figure in the Liberal Party. When the party had failed to put up a candidate for a by-election in the constituency in November 1896 he intervened to find a candidate, Billson, to oppose the ILP leader, Keir Hardie. This action finally demonstrated the extent to which Illingworth - a supposed 'Radical' Liberal politician - was opposed to organised Labour. It gave rise to a withering critique in the *Daily Chronicle* describing 'Illingworthism' as 'a gospel without sympathy, comradeship, or hope for the Bradford worker, and an attempt to identify it with Liberalism has had its consequences in Kier Hardeism.'

Asked whether he supported the eight hour day (in an interview on Labour Questions for the *Bradford Observer* in May 1892) Isaac replied, "It would be our ruin – at least until the Germans and the French, our great competitors, reduced their hours to something like those which we have in this country. An hour's work a day may give the manufacturer his profit." However he then added, "In the case of the miner there is a danger and there is injury to health. They are shut out from the light of day. The more their hours are limited the better." Unsurprisingly in view of these comments, Isaac was roundly criticised at a meeting in Victoria Park in Keighley for voting against the Bill; he had previously intimated support for the principle of the Bill at a meeting with Trades Council and ILP representatives.

Death Duties

William Harcourt, the Chancellor of the Exchequer, included the introduction of an inheritance tax in his 1894 Budget. While estates had paid inheritance taxes before, the new death duties introduced a potentially confiscatory attitude towards inheritance. The controversial proposal and other provisions of the budget were debated over three months. On May 10th 1894 Isaac spoke in the Budget debate and began by saying he 'seldom troubled the House with his oratory because he was a plain man of business and did not go outside what he considered to be his business duties, but he could not allow this opportunity to pass without expressing his entire approval for the very moderate and rational and democratic Budget which the Chancellor of the Exchequer had submitted to the House.' He went on:

> 'What ever might be said against the death duties as unjustly oppressing the landed classes, it must be remembered the class was limited, and in no country in the world was the soil held in the hands of so few persons as in this country. There could be no doubt that the working classes of this country, who were a very large majority, looked upon the greatly increased wealth of the commercial and industrial men and the great landlord proprietors of this country and considered that property was very unequally distributed. This Budget was the beginning of a new state of affairs'.

Isaac added that he and others had derived a large amount of wealth from the woolcombing industry adding, 'the inventions which they had patented had the effect that some thirty of forty workers could now do the work of 3,000 men, who would be employed on it but for the substitution of machinery. They in these industries did not complain of having to pay the graduated income tax, because they could never have made any profits out of their inventions without the protection which had been given to them by the Government. They obtained a monopoly for fourteen years and ought to pay for the privilege.' William Harcourt later wrote a personal note thanking Isaac, 'I shall always remember that nothing did more to secure the passing of the Budget than the admirable speech which you delivered on the second reading, and which coming from you carried with it so much weight.'

The *Daily Chronicle* remarked:

> 'A rather unlooked for, but very welcome appearance in last night's debate on the Budget Bill was that of Sir Isaac Holden. The hon. baronet is eighty seven years of age, is a manufacturer on a very large scale, both in England and France, a prolific inventor, and one of the wealthiest men in the House, which is saying a great deal. He spoke excellently for about a quarter of an hour, and gave cordial approval to a Budget, which one day, may it be far distant, will tax his millions up to eight per cent'.

However, in a speech in Arbroath that October, Kier Hardie derided Isaac's reference in his Budget speech to the effect that some thirty of forty workers could now do the work of 3,000 men. In fairness in his speech Kier Hardie had taken these words out of context, as Isaac had actually been referring to the profits entrepreneurs made out of their inventions thanks to patent protection and that they ought to pay tax for the privilege.

Nevertheless, in a letter to the Editor of the Pall Mall Gazette on May 22nd a correspondent also questioned why Isaac, whilst boasting in his Budget speech that the mechanisation of Woolcombing meant thirty of forty workers could now do the work of 3,000 men, had voted for a Bill for the exemption of machinery from rates which could have been used for the relief of the 2,960 men and women that mechanisation had rendered unemployed.

Rights, liberty and independence

The following year Isaac made some notes in preparation for a speech he was to give in his constituency on his retirement. He wrote: 'the animus of my public life in politics – rights, liberty and independence'; collectivism would destroy liberty tomorrow without individualism.' In expressing his belief in individualism and individual rights in these terms Isaac is aligning himself to the ideal of Benthamite individualism, which saw the responsibility of the legislator as being to give free scope to the intelligence and enterprise of the individual, in opposition to the rising tide of collectivism. A belief in free trade, the emancipation of slaves and religious equality are all examples of the individualistic policies Isaac had advocated during his political life. The 1870 Education Act contained collectivist redistributive principles by providing for those who could not or would not educate children from their own resources. However Isaac's motive for supporting the Education Act had been essentially individualistic. His predominant concern had been to secure non-denominational religious instruction untrammelled by the power and doctrine of the Church of England.

In the preparatory speech notes Isaac summed up his business philosophy as being 'competition, individuality, responsibility, invention and patents.' As an entrepreneur and free trader he, in common with other prominent radicals from a manufacturing background, was generally resistant to state interference or regulation of industry. For example, he took part in a 'deputation of masters' to the Home Office to oppose the Nine Hours Bill, and later voted against the Miners' Eight Hours Bill. The notes also suggest that he was resolutely opposed to collectivist demands from the rapidly growing trade unions for wage rises beyond what he saw as prevailing conditions: 'Trades unions will tend to equalisation of conditions in industries which is desirable to employers as much as to the workman at home but the same conditions must exist among our foreign competitors.'

The *Keighley Daily News* reported Isaac speaking at a meeting in Howarth on his retirement from parliament in the following terms:

'As a young man he heartily joined in the agitation for Catholic emancipation, and for the great Reform Bill of 1832; he was present in the House of Commons at one of the debates on the liberation of slaves; he took a long and deep interest in the abolition of the Corn Laws; he spoke three-quarters of an hour in favour of giving the franchise to £7 rentals; and on the abolition of church rates he spoke at the request of Mr. Gladstone, who took a lively interest in the question. He took part in the debate and in the division for the disestablishment of the Irish Church. He had also joined in passing many subsequent acts'.

His political career thus reflected the pursuit of causes he held in common with other radical Nonconformist Liberals: beginning with the reform of the Corn Laws, the extension of the franchise and the abolition of rotten boroughs, and the efforts to limit the power of the established church including church rates, and Irish Home Rule.

He now repaired to Oakworth to spend his final days. Perhaps in the light of the continuing difficulties over Edward's finances and the substantial cash injection he had made to bail him out, in 1896 he made a dramatic alteration to his Will. Under his earlier Will the estate was to have been divided into four equal parts. Each of his two daughters was to have had their shares held in a trust 'free from the control of her husband'. Now he inserted a Codicil stating, 'Instead of bequeathing to my sons equal portions of my estate I by this codicil bequeath to each of my daughters Mary and Margaret double what I bequeath to my sons Angus and Edward.' So far as the business was concerned, which was to have been left in control of his sons, he now instructed them in the codicil to "pay in cash (as much as they will be able to raise) to their sisters and what they may not be able to pay (in) cash to pay by shares in the company.' Given that most of Isaac's capital was actually tied up in the company this latter caveat was very valuable to the daughters.

Fittingly Margaret was an early suffragette. Her father had voted in support of JS Mill's amendment to the 1867 Reform Bill for the enfranchisement of women and her husband, Alfred Illingworth, had supported the Married Women's Property Act (1893) giving married women legal control of all the property they inherited or by their own earnings. Margaret's protected inheritance now gave her the means and the independence to support the suffragette cause. After meeting her in 1899 Elizabeth Wolstenholme Elmy recruited her to the cause: 'she is rich intelligent and kind hearted. She is quite able, if only we could stir her up to the point, to do great things financially for the women's cause, since I suppose she has somewhat over half a million at her disposal.' Margaret joined the Women's Franchise League and then the Women's Emancipation Union. In 1910 she gave her support to the Tax Resistance League, a direct action group which refused to pay taxes as part of the struggle for women's suffrage, and went on to become the president of Bradford's Women's Suffrage Society, and the vice president of both the National Women's Suffrage Societies and the London Society for Women's Suffrage.

In another clause in Isaac's earlier Will Sarah, who predeceased him, was to have been permitted to take from his wine cellar only such portions thereof as shall be required for actual consumption'. After he died his gross estate (excluding his share of the business which, of course, counted for most of his wealth) was £315,883 (£29 million in today's terms) and after the death duties at 8 per cent and other dispersals were taken into account was £254,059.

Isaac's obituaries published at the time of his death suggested that it was well known he had given away up to £2 million to family members in the years before he died. If this is true it may well have been to avoid the death duties applicable because of the Act he had played a role in passing. He certainly bailed out Edward to a significant degree. He made other more personal gifts to other family members during this period, including of a college rowing boat to his grandson, Percy Illingworth, at Jesus College Cambridge (the restrictions on Nonconformists being admitted being one of the Bills he had voted for in parliament) and a colt for his niece, Clara, who had been his housekeeper at Queen Anne's Mansions during his last session in parliament. Clara, who was very close to her grandfather, wrote him many letters including one telling him she had been to Chamanoix and had climbed 'to an altitude of 13,000 feet. Most of the time was steep snow. We were roped together for 6 hours'. Percy Illingworth served in the second Boer War as a trooper in the Yorkshire Hussars. In 1906 he was returned to Parliament for Shipley and he was to go on to serve as a Parliamentary Secretary to the Treasury alongside Lloyd George and then the Liberal Chief whip in Asquith's Government in 1912. He died of food poisoning from a bad oyster in 1915.

Isaac died at the age of 90 on August 13th 1897 with his children by his bedside. He had been driving in a carriage on the moors the day before he died. A funeral service was held in the chapel at Oakworth where the minister Mr. Christian spoke of Isaac as 'to the end the same gentle, modest, sympathetic man, there was summer always about him, a winsomeness, a serenity of disposition, and that told of a quiet, untroubled mind'. The mile long funeral cortege included nineteen carriages carrying family members and friends and four conveyances of wreaths. It progressed through Keighley and Bingley to Bradford, where the Mayor of Bradford, local dignitaries, and a thousand employees of Isaac's firm met it on the Queen's Road. Thousands more lined the route and local traders drew their shop blinds in respect. After the hymn, 'Jesus lover of my Soul' was sung at the graveside, the coffin was interned in the Undercliffe cemetery.

The Grand Old Man

Several obituaries referred to Isaac as being the 'GOM of Yorkshire' (Grand Old Man) and heaped praise on his life. This seems to have been enough to stir up his old sparring partner's long felt animosity. On August 21st Lister, now Lord Masham, wrote a vituperative letter to the Editor of the Engineer responding to its positive obituary published just the day before:

> *'At last that wonderful man, Sir Isaac Holden, has joined the great majority, and the story of his life is now before the public and it seems a pity to spoil so pleasant and entertaining story as that given to us by the public press… But biography to be worth anything should give us facts, and not fiction, although it might not be so amusing..'*

Yet again Lister went on to refute Isaac's clams to be the inventor of the Square Motion woolcombing machine, writing several letters to other papers in a similar vein. He also alleged that Donnisthorpe had defrauded him by selling him 'the worthless patent of 1842'. Doubtless induced to do so by Lister, Jonathan Holden, who had been mentioned in Lister's letter, now wrote claiming credit for having modified the Square Motion machine and making it work in the early days at St. Denis (*Sheffield Daily Telegraph*, September 20th 1897).

Donnisthorpe's son, Wordsworth, subsequently wrote a strong letter of rebuke to the papers:

> 'Although Lord Masham's outrageous letter put him outside the pale of courteous argument, and although it might be more becoming to maintain a dignified silence, like that observed by all the members of the late Sir Isaac Holden's family, after the vulgar and scurrilous attacks made upon him before his grave has closed, still I feel that if I failed to answer some of his charges and taunts I should be guilty of injustice to my late father'.

Wordsworth Donnisthorpe went on to mount a staunch defence of his father. [Wordsworth Donnisthorpe developed the Kinesigraph camera, which was inspired by the square motion machine with the "falling combs" replaced by falling photographic plates "to facilitate the taking of a succession of photographs at equal intervals in time". He patented the camera with his cousin, William Carr Crofts, and they used the camera to shoot a short film of Trafalgar Square in 1891 (cited in Herbert, Stephen, Industry, Liberty and a Vision: Wordsworth Donnisthorpe's Kinesigraph, London, The Projection Box 1998)].

Samuel Lister, Lord Masham, died on February 2nd 1906 after catching influenza at his home, Swinton Castle, at the age of 91 and is buried in the family vault at Addingham.

Angus Holden inherited the Baronetcy after Isaac's death and having served as a Liberal MP for Bradford East from 1885-86 and then for Buckrose from 1892-1900 he was raised to the peerage in 1908 as Baron Holden of Alston in Cumberland. He had moved a long way from his views on the peerage and the reform of the House of Lords in his electoral address of 1885, 'The hereditary principle is out of harmony with the spirit of the age'. His grandson, Lord Angus Holden, joined the Labour Party in 1945 having served in the Second World War as a naval officer. He served as Under Secretary of State for Commonwealth Relations in Clem Atlee's Labour Government.

Endnotes

The Isaac Holden archives are split between the Papers of Sir Isaac Holden and Family in the Special Collections of the J.B. Priestley Library at the University of Bradford and the Isaac Holden and Sons Ltd., Business Records in the Special Collections at the Brotherton Library at Leeds University. Both sets of papers were donated by Isaac's great-grandson, Sir Edward Holden. Quotations from these sources are listed under the appropriate chapter number in the Sources section below as either, JBPL and the relevant Bundle number for the J.B. Priestley Library, or, BL and the relevant box number for the Brotherton Library.

Percy Lund, Humphries and Co., Ltd published the Holden Illingworth Letters in Bradford in 1927. Fred Byles, and A.J. Best, acting under the supervision of Isaac's grandson, Eustace. H. Illingworth compiled the letters. The letters from which they are edited form part of the archives at Bradford and Leeds Universities. Their use in the Holden Illingworth Letters is selective and partial, but they are accurately reproduced. When the Holden Illingworth Letters are referred to in the Sources section they are tagged as HIL.

Eustace Illingworth kept Sarah and Isaac's courtship correspondence, together with some election posters and family photographs, in a separate metal box and these were not used in the Holden Illingworth Letters. Sir Edward Holden, who withheld its contents from the papers given to the two universities, inherited the metal box. The box came into my hands on his death and will be donated to Bradford University.

Katrina Honeyman and Jordan Goodman undertook a case study, The late Technology and Enterprise: Isaac Holden and the Mechanisation of Woolcombing in France 1848-1914., Scolar Press, 1986, which drew on the Leeds and Bradford archives, They also examined and analyzed papers held by members of the family, Annie and Annette Bywater and Janet Gough, as well as French archives in Châlons sur-Marne and Lille. This biography draws on their excellent analysis of the development and diffusion of wool combing technology in and by the Lister and Holden enterprise.

Eric. M. Sigsworth undertook a study of Isaac Holden, Sir Isaac Holden Bt.: First Comber in Europe, which in a shortened version (p. 339-353) is published in Textile and Economic History; Essays in Honour of Miss Julia de Lacy Mann., Manchester University Press 1973. I have drawn on elements of this study in this biography.

Elizabeth Jennings, who undertook a PhD thesis, Sir Isaac Holden(1807-1897) at Bradford University in 1982, has written Sir Isaac Holden, Bart; his place in the Wesleyan Connexion' in the Proceedings of the Wesley Historical Society 43, 1982, pages 117-126 and 150-190. Her work has enabled me to place Isaac's Nonconformity beliefs and actions in the Wesleyan context.

John Tosh, who has written extensively on masculinity and gender in Victorian society, wrote, From Keighley to St Denis: separation and intimacy in Victorian bourgeoisie marriage, History Workshop Journal 40, 1995 pp. 193-206. His work has informed some of what is written in this biography about Isaacs's marriage and role as a parent.

To understand and put in context Isaac's involvement as an entrepreneur in the hot house of Bradford and West Yorkshire's radical nonconformist Liberal Party politics in the second half of the Nineteenth Century I have drawn particularly upon: Entrepreneurial Politics in Mid-Victorian Britain, G.R. Searle, Oxford University Press 1992; Class Formation and Urban Industrial Society, Bradford 1750-1850, Theodore Koditschek, Cambridge University Press, 1990; Patrick Joyce, Work Society and Politics, The culture of the factory in later Victorian England, Methuen 1982; J.P. Parry, Democracy & Religion, Gladstone and the Liberal Party 1867-1875, Cambridge University Press, 1986; Patrick Jackson, Education Act Forster, A political biography of W.E. Forster (1818-1886), Associated University Presses, 1997; Arthur Miall, Life of Edward Miall' formerly Member of Parliament for Rochdale and Bradford, 1884 reproduced by Ulan Press.

Anyone who wants to gain an understanding of the social conditions and hardships brought about in Bradford as a result of the mechanisation of wool combing should read, Mechanization and Misery, The Bradford Woolcombers Report of 1845, with an introduction by J.A. Jowittt, Ryburn Archive Editions, 1991. And to understand the factors which led to the emergence of the Independent Labour Party in Bradford: Jonathan Schneer, Ben Tillett, Croom Helm Ltd printed by Billing and Sons, 1982; Fenner Brockway, Socialism over Sixty Years, George Allen & Unwin, 1946.

Descendents of Isaac Haldan

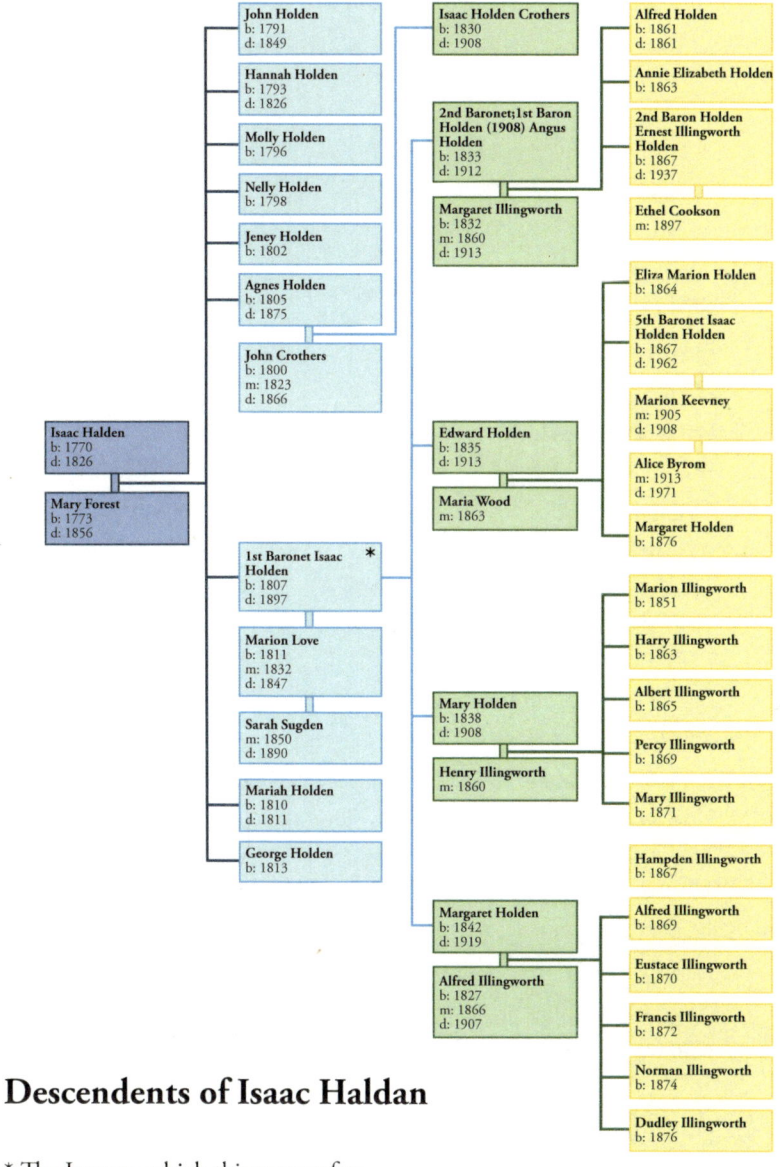

Isaac Halden b: 1770, d: 1826
Mary Forest b: 1773, d: 1856

- **John Holden** b: 1791, d: 1849
- **Hannah Holden** b: 1793, d: 1826
- **Molly Holden** b: 1796
- **Nelly Holden** b: 1798
- **Jeney Holden** b: 1802
- **Agnes Holden** b: 1805, d: 1875
  - **John Crothers** b: 1800, m: 1823, d: 1866
    - **Isaac Holden Crothers** b: 1830, d: 1908
- **1st Baronet Isaac Holden** * b: 1807, d: 1897
  - **Marion Love** b: 1811, m: 1832, d: 1847
  - **Sarah Sugden** m: 1850, d: 1890
    - **2nd Baronet; 1st Baron Holden (1908) Angus Holden** b: 1833, d: 1912
      - **Margaret Illingworth** b: 1832, m: 1860, d: 1913
        - **Alfred Holden** b: 1861, d: 1861
        - **Annie Elizabeth Holden** b: 1863
        - **2nd Baron Holden Ernest Illingworth Holden** b: 1867, d: 1937
          - **Ethel Cookson** m: 1897
    - **Edward Holden** b: 1835, d: 1913
      - **Maria Wood** m: 1863
        - **Eliza Marion Holden** b: 1864
        - **5th Baronet Isaac Holden Holden** b: 1867, d: 1962
          - **Marion Keevney** m: 1905, d: 1908
          - **Alice Byrom** m: 1913, d: 1971
        - **Margaret Holden** b: 1876
    - **Mary Holden** b: 1838, d: 1908
      - **Henry Illingworth** m: 1860
        - **Marion Illingworth** b: 1851
        - **Harry Illingworth** b: 1863
        - **Albert Illingworth** b: 1865
        - **Percy Illingworth** b: 1869
        - **Mary Illingworth** b: 1871
    - **Margaret Holden** b: 1842, d: 1919
      - **Alfred Illingworth** b: 1827, m: 1866, d: 1907
        - **Hampden Illingworth** b: 1867
        - **Alfred Illingworth** b: 1869
        - **Eustace Illingworth** b: 1870
        - **Francis Illingworth** b: 1872
        - **Norman Illingworth** b: 1874
        - **Dudley Illingworth** b: 1876
- **Mariah Holden** b: 1810, d: 1811
- **George Holden** b: 1813

* The Isaac to which this story refers.

191

Sources

Chapter One.

1. the Corn Laws, the petitions of the State clergy, Memoir of John Fraser, James Fraser, 1879

2. being chosen and acted as a Committee who commanded a mob … on 3rd April, Dodsley's Annual Register(1820), Part 1, page 343

3. a puny little child, too feeble to go to school in winter, Character Sketches: Sir Isaac Holden. Review of Reviews, Emily Crawford

4. he hoped hereafter he would gladly incur dismissal for any good cause, Character Sketches: Sir Isaac Holden. Review of Reviews, Emily Crawford

5. two of the most distinguished radicals of the time, *Bradford Observer* January 1st 1894

6. quite blithe and hauty like, , Mrs Halden to Isaac April 1st 1828, The Holden Illingworth Letters (HIL) Page 4

7. One thing dear brother … your attachment in Paisley is reciprocal, E. McLerie to Isaac, 1829, HIL Page 11,

8. I see no beauty in the shining day, Love Poem by Isaac Holden, HIL Page 22

9. he was prepared to incur the displeasure of the patron rather than part with me, interview with Sir Isaac Holden *Leeds Mercury*, 27th March 1892

10. rather strong spelks and were not vey inflammable, Isaac to Joshua Parrott, 11th April 1895. J.B. Priestley Library (JBPL),

11. were but a happy thought without an expenditure of time and money to mature, January 1st 1894, *Bradford Observer*

12. Young Gentleman engaged in the Counting House, HIL Page 21

13. It is now five years since my more intimate acquaintance with her, IH to Mr and Mrs Love , HIL Page 26,

14. Several hundreds of men are daily employed breaking up stones in a quarry, James Riley to IH, HIL Page 35

15. an association among private members of our body, IH to John Kennedy, HIL Page 50

Chapter 2.

16. I conceive you to be bound to obtain before proceeding to construct such machinery, John Kennedy to IH, HIL Page 55,

17. to address themselves to actions not words, IH to the Editor of the *Sun*, HIL Page 97

18. would be communicated by the idle Bishops, whose lessons would resemble their sermons, HIL Page 99

19. Require them to apologise for the unmerited charges, IH Notebook 1844, Box 2 Brotherton Library (BL)

20. indiscriminate anti patent principle may lead to our separation, IH notebook 1845, Bundle 6 BL

21. the flame flickering on the surface where gas was bubbling out, 7 March 1850, *Bradford Observer*,

22. I don't feel right unless I am always thinking about you and home, Marion

23. Holden to Isaac, June 17, 1845, Box 6, Bundle 6, BL

24. She died in the full triumph of the Faith, IH to Wm. Craven, HIL Page 125,

25. paid Betty Ackroyd £1 for attending to my poor late wife, 20 May 1847, IH Notebook. 1846-49,

Chapter 3.

1. Memorandum of Agreement a taking out joint patent, 1847, JBPL
2. The apparently complementary aims of the two partners, Technology and Enterprise: Isaac Holden and the Mechanisation of Woolcombing in France 1848-1914, Katrina Honeyman and Jordan Goodman, Scolar Press
3. if you can take a place out of town it would be better, Lister to IH, 25 September 1848, Bundle 1/4/2 JBPL
4. Partnership deed with Lister, 22 July 1847, Bundle 1/4/1 JBPL
5. Reducing his initial capital outlay from £3000 £2000, SCL to IH, 1st November 1848. Bundle 1/4/2 JPBL.
6. you are a lucky man to have the chance of a third of such a business, SCL to IH, July 3 1849, Bundle 1/4/3 JBPL

Chapters 4.

1. Having no inclination to keep your mind in suspense, Sarah Sugden to Isaac Holden, May 1848, Box 6, Brotherton Library
2. The 'courtship letters' private collection (to be donated to the J. B. Priestley Library, Bradford University)

Chapter 5.

26. I am going to engage the sister of Mr Field, our second preacher as governess, Courtship letters.
27. Such a large sum expended in making a beginning is to me incomprehensible, SCL to IH, 30 May 1849, Bundle 1/4/3, JBPL.
28. The whole of the workpeople entering the gates in procession, Sarah Holden to IH, HIL
29. You seem to be so much happier with your brothers and among your old friends than with me, IH to Sarah, July 10 1851, Bundle 1/2/1 JBPL

30. A kind of parlour border, Mary Holden to IH, Summer 1855, Bundle 6, Box 7, BL

31. It is very thoughtless of him. All the ladies went home yesterday. Mary to IH, 22nd June 1855, Box 7 BL

32. another time we shall be more stringent, Miss Watts to IH, 25 April 1857, Bundle 8, Box 7, BL

33. Your future happiness depends much on a well cultivated mind, IH to Maggie, June 10th 1858, Bundle 3/1/2 JBPL

34. I should like you to see us at our gymnastics, Maggie Holden to IH, April 6 1860. Bundle 1, Box 8, BL

35. "Be cheerful and gay and throw yourself without fear into al the innocent hilarity of good society, chase way gloom as a vitiating and dangerous thing". IH to Sarah, 21 June 1852, HIL.

36. I conclude it was only a slip of the pen. IH to Sarah. 10 July 1850, Bundle 1/2/2. JBPL.

37. 'better satisfied with France', Jonas Sugden to IH, 28 April 1851, Bundle 1/2/3. JBPL.

38. as to choosing one of my own ranks, there are but a few of the young ladies of the present day that bring much profit with them, William Craven to Jonas Sugden, July 1853, Bundle 2/1/2 JBPL

39. my feelings for you ensure against all judgement of the mind induces me to try another time, Sarah to William Craven, 18 October 1856, Bundle 2/1/2 JBPL

40. I am not teetotal, but on that hand am very much improved, William Craven to Sarah, December 21, 1857, Bundle 2/1/2 JBPL

41. Let me recommend religion - don't be jealous, IH Memorandum Book 1856-57, BL

42. Altogether Tavernier has shown too much apathy. IH Notebook 1850/51, Bundle 4/2/1 JBPL

43. sell up every shillings worth of stock, Lister to IH, 24 May 1851, Bundle 1/4/4. JBPL.

44. shameful, Lister to IH, 26 July 1851, Bundle 1/4/4 JBPL
45. Have you lost £19,000 in half a year? Lister to IH, 30 July 1851, Bundle 1/4/4. JBPL
46. We are now all quiet here and at Paris. IH to Sarah, December 7th 1851, HIL
47. Napoleon desires much to ameliorate the conditions of the lower classes. IH to Sarah, 21 December 1851, HIL
48. After you had, at least for the time, laid it aside as useless for fine wool, I took it out of the corner, December 25th 1851, Bundle 1/4/4 JBPL
49. Lister first proposed that the share holdings be redistributed. Bundle 1/4/6 JBPL
50. A suitable girl for a wife, IH to Sarah, 22 August 1853, HIL page 180
51. There are some reports flying around about the Russians entering Turkey and that war is certain. Lister to IH, 20 June 1853, Bundle 1/4/5 JBPL
52. What annoys and vexes me is that I made a special journey to France, Lister to IH, 31 December 1853, Bundle 1/4/5 JBPL
53. I have £70,000 in the French concern and not been able to get a shilling is a rascally shame, Lister to IH, 25 June 1854, Bundle 1/4/6 JBPL
54. Mr Lister is going to be married to a very wealthy lady, IH to Sarah, 2nd August 1854, Bundle 1/2/5 JBPL
55. It is worth little to Brothers and it is worth 5 per cent at least to us, IH to Sarah, 1 September 1854, Bundle 1/2/5 JBPL
56. While we were in a little hazard owing to Mr Lister's indiscreet outlay of capital, IH to Jonas Sugden, 1 September 1854, Bundle 1/2/5 JBPL
57. I am not a little harassed with some nasty affairs in business, the result of Tavernier's conduct, IH to Sarah, 6 September 1854, Bundle 1/2/5 JBPL
58. Tavernier threatens to commence action. Note in September 1854 in IH Notebook, July 1854 to July 1855, JBPL

59. Tavernier like a little tom fool comes bobbing in every morning swishing his wig. Angus Holden to IH, 10 August 1854, Bundle 1/4/6 JBPL

60. Dear Sir, by superior orders of Mr Holden, I must not send you any money. Tavernier to Lister, 3 November 1854, Bundle 1/4/6 JBPL

61. Your conduct is abominable ... I will put an end to the partnership, Lister to IH, 6 November 1854, Bundle 1/4/6 JBPL

62. if he will have Tavernier he must part with you, Jonas Sugden to IH, 26 December 1854, Bundle 1/4/6 JBPL

63. Be very cautious what you do with these scoundrels, IH to Lister, 13 June 1855, Bundle 1/4/7 JBPL

64. It appears the Baron has changed his mind or his friends did for him, Lister to IH, 20 June 1855, Bundle 1/4/7 JBPL

65. It is in both Donnisthorpe and Tavernier's interest to help you if you do not provoke them, Lister to IH, August 5th 1855, Bundle 1/4/7 JBPL

66. The scene of that day at the Palais de Justice in ineffaceably fixed on my mental retina, David Gunton to IH, August 7 1855, Bundle 5, Box 7, Brotherton Library

67. I know how to appreciate Tavernier's help and honesty, IH to Lister, 9 August 1855, Bundle 1/4/7 JBPL

68. a few of the leading facts which I hope you will read to your wife, Lister to IH, 19 October 1855, Bundle 1/4/7 JBPL

69. Should show letters… and also Mr Lister's letter in which he speaks of buying off Donnisthorpe. Entry dated 17 November 1855 in IH Notebook 1855-56, JBPL

70. Mr Lister seems to see clearly he cannot attain his objective by the course he has adopted. IH to Sarah, 27 October 1855, HIL

Chapter 6.

1. The authorities of Reims are making much ado about our suds, Jonathan Holden to Isaac, 16 June 1856, HIL

2. In some things they have gone further than I would and in others I would have bought something finer, IH to Sarah, 22 March 1858, HIL

3. I hereby engage to drink no brandy, wine, beer of fermented liquors, Box 1, BL

4. If I knew that we had any men that conversed or interfered in politics, Jonathan Holden to Isaac, November 7 1856, HIL

5. The Emperor spoke like a man having authority, Isaac to Sarah, November 16, 1855, HIL

6. I must tell you we had a beautiful view of the Emperor and Empress, Mary to Maggie Holden, February 19th 1858. Bundle 3/1/2 JBPL

7. If he is not wishful to sell to you, wait till all gets in the hands of the creditors, Angus Holden to IH, December 1857, Bundle 8, Box 7, BL

8. The most scandalous fraud… they sell to me an agreement without explaining to me in any way its contents, Lister to IH, March 27 1857, Bundle 1/4/9, JBPL

9. I think I shall earn the character of a regular "Boxer at Law", SCL to IH, 9 March 1858, Bundle 1/4/10 JBPL

10. I prefer to have less risk in France. SCL to IH, 1 October 1858, Bundle 1/4/10 JBPL

11. Tavernier is going swaggering that he is in again with Lister, Angus to IH, 5 October 1858, Bundle 9, Box 7, BL

12. I suppose I have bought the whole French business on good terms which I shall explain when I see you. Isaac to Sarah, November 9 1858, HIL

13. I have been incessantly occupied from morning to night, Isaac to Sarah, November 5 1858, HIL

14. This morning an Englishman set out for the ascent (of Mont Blanc), Angus to Isaac, 9 September 1858, HIL

Chapter 7.

1. I fear much whether ever you (will) acquire those minutious and careful, painstaking habits, Isaac to Angus, March 12 1859, HIL

2. not to form expensive habits before you are worth something, Isaac to Angus, December 22 1859. Holden Illingworth Letters.

3. Poor dear father, I do pity him that old creature, Mary to Margaret Holden, September 13 1860, Bundle 3/1/2 JBPL

4. All much as usual St Dennis the same dismal hole – old Madam just the same, Angus to Margaret Holden, 18 February 1859, Bundle 3/1/2 JBPL

5. An Englishman is worthless unless he is an accomplished French scholar, 28 September 1861, HIL

6. the vast progress which you have made in the short space of twenty months fills us with hope that every stain on your freedom, Public Meeting, Free Trade Hall, Manchester, 31 December 1862

7. We shall have to decide when you come back about the height of the chimney, Angus to Isaac, August 26 1864, HIL

8. French ladies discovered that light woollens were safer to war in the chill of the evening than muslin or cotton, Character sketches Sir Isaac Holden, Emily Crawford.

9. The carding machines are kept running night and day, two relays of work-people being employed, James Burnley, The Alston Wool-combing Works of Messrs, Isaac Holden and Sons at Bradford, in Great Industries of Great Britain, 1884, published by Casell, Petter and Galpin

Chapter 8.

1. La! Turned half past 8 pm in our squat little study, Angus Holden to Margaret, HIL

2. I always was and always shall be a poor beggar where my own interests are concerned, Maggie Holden to Isaac, 25 June 1867, Bundle 1/1/10 JPBL

3. Poor dear father, I do pity him that old creature, for I know he is miserable with her, he cannot be otherwise, Mary to Maggie Holden, September 13 1860, Bundle 3/1/2 JBPL

4. All much as usual St Dennis the same dismal hole – old Madam just the same as she always was, Angus Holden to Maggie, 18 February 1859, Bundle 3/1/2 JBPL

5. Have you forgotten our last drive to Paris in the Voiture de Ville, Henry Illingworth to Maggie Holden, 9 October 1860, Bundle 3/1/2 JBPL

6. The leeches applied on Mary's chest did her much good, Bundle 1/1/4 JBPL

7. Have things boxed up a little. I wish you and Mother would make a few necessary purchases without further delay. Margaret Holden to Isaac, May 3rd 1864, HIL

8. I still punish myself by my unconquerable desire to effect economies. IH to Angus Love, 1865, Box 5/5 BL

9. It is a fine building… I wish we had one in England, IH

10. a magnificent place, containing almost all that the heart of a man could desire, save a dog, John Bright, 30 September 1898, *Manchester Times*

Chapter 9.

1. The whole thing is a stupendous money making scheme carried out under false pretences, cited in G. Kitson Clark, An Expanding Society: Britain 1830-1900.

2. Those foolish people who have put in the Pontefract paper that you had accepted, Bundle 1/1/6 JBPL

3. at feasts, fairs and other worldly amusements, Commerce and Christianity, Memorial of Jonas Sugden (London 1857)

4. Eastbrook chapel is proceeding very satisfactorily and we shall have it ready in plenty of time for the opening, Angus to Isaac, August 26 1863, HIL

5. Mr Holden shewed me some parts of Paris, in order to give me some idea how the Sabbath was spent, Sarah Holden to Jonas Sugden, Box 4, BL

6. A feeble voice has a chance to be heard, Isaac Holden to A. McAuley, 5 January 1871, Letter Book, JBPL

7. Excluding forever the use of Liturgy, Rev. J. Mayer to Isaac Holden, 10 January 1866, Box 8/5 BL

8. We want no better book of praise than the Wesleyan hymnbook. R. Gascoyne to Isaac, 27 June 1869, Box 7b, BL

9. glad to find that your losses are £40,000 less than Mr. Angus estimated them, 6 June 1871, Sir Francis Lycett to IH, HIL

10. I think the best thing you can do in London is to increase the number of humbler Meeting Houses, IH to Sir Francis Lycett, 27 June 1871, HIL

11. I notice that among all the new buildings that cover your once wild hills, churches and schools are … almost always Gothic, Ruskin's lecture Traffic on the opening of the Wool Exchange 1864

12. feeble imitation of the Establishment… will open out the sympathy of many of our people, IH to Rev William Arthur, June 28 1871, HIL

13. it appears very remarkable that the owner and occupier of a burgage house has not the vote, Baines, *Yorks. Dir.* (1822), ii. 223; *PP* (1831), xvi. 105.

14. ought to be tied to a cart and be publicly whipped, Isaac Holden reported in the Leeds Mercury, 14 July 1865

15. The men, who by a large majority of voted, and by an immense preponderance of the intelligence, the respectability, and the Property of this Borough, Election poster 1865, Bundle 1/1/11 JBPL

16. During the last eventful Thirty-five years though closely engaged in business, Election poster 1865, Private Collection

17. Shame! Shame! On the individuals, Men of Landed Property, Election poster 1865, Private Collection

18. In Memory of Briefless Tom, Election leaflet, Private Collection

19. Knaresboro' yesterday as the scene of the keenest contest which the recent election has produced, Newspaper article cited in Holden Illingworth Letters.
20. to place before you our exact position as regards the heavy debts of our chapel property, Methodist Ministers to IH, January 8 1866, Box 8, Brotherton Library
21. The doctor says my head will take some time to cure, IH to Sarah, November 18 1866, HIL
22. I was more delighted by the fact that the money was chiefly raised by working men, March 28 1866, HIL
23. the representative of one of the condemned boroughs, 1 June 1866, *Hansard*.
24. Knaresborough was one of the smallest boroughs in the kingdom in point of area, 22 June 1867, *Hansard*
25. He knew the town of Knaresborough well, 22 June 1867, *Hansard*
26. They would not have objected to the income derived from fixed sources—such as tithe—being continued to the Church. 1 August 1866, *Hansard*
27. We will have settled pretty nearly all of the previous Knaresboro incidents of this description, Angus Holden to IH, 16 July 1873, Bundle 1/1/7 JBPL
28. Why? Because we believe it to be unjust, The Liberation Society: its policy and motives, J. Mial, 1859
29. They would not have objected to the income derived from fixed sources, Isaac Holden, 1 August 1866, *Hansard*
30. If you prevent any but a strictly religious employment of the Sunday, J.S. Mill, 1 August 1866, *Hansard*
31. Coming into the House I asked an hon. Member how he would vote, John Bright, 1 August 1866, *Hansard*
32. protested against its going forth to the public that they legislated in this House on religious, Isaac Holden, 1 August 1866, *Hansard*

33. Mr. Gladstone was at this time in his politics a liberal reformer of Turgot's type, John Morley, *The Life of William Ewart Gladstone*

34. use your influence with him to entirely abandon any idea of entering parliament, Margaret Holden to IH, 7 August 1868, HIL

35. a grand demonstration in my park when Forster and Miall will be present, Angus Holden to IH, May 20, 1869, HIL

36. in favour of the Gladstone policy for the man who, in the House of Commons, would support that policy, IH to the Editor of the *Watchman*, 1868

37. Mr and Mrs Miall are staying with us – party after party, Margaret Holden to Isaac, July 1867, Bundle 1/1/8 JBPL

38. Mr Miall's presence in the House of Commons is found now to be a national want, *Life of Edward Miall*, formerly Member of Parliament for Rochdale and Bradford, Arthur Miall 1884

39. household suffrage, not hampered and restrained by the personal payment of rates, *Life of Edward Miall*

40. What do you say to the elections in the factory districts? Once again the proletariat has discredited itself terribly, Engels to Marx, November 18, 1868, *Marx and Engels Correspondence*.

41. the logical way to solve the religious education difficulty, IH notebook 1858 JBPL, 4/2/1

42. national education, supported by rates and national funds, of purely secular education, Isaac Holden April 8 1870, Letter to the Editors of the *Leeds Mercury*

43. I had no wish to injure dissent nor to do it any good, and I had no wish to injure the Church nor to do it any good. I simply wanted to get the children to school. W.E. Forster27 November 1873, *Manchester Guardian*

44. References to Isaac and Sarah's trio to the Holy Land, Letters to his Children on his journey to the Holy Land, published by I.H. Illingworth in 1957, JBPL

Chapter 10.

1. on a drive to the Bois de Boulogne, IH to Sarah, 18 August 1870, HIL
2. by the usual train and in the usual time, IH to Sarah, 20 August 1870, HIL
3. making yourself into a hermit. I am doing nothing of the kind, IH to Sarah, 25 August 1870, HIL
4. There have been great military movements going on since we came. IH to Sarah, 26 August 1870, HIL
5. him and our affairs in the care of kind providence. IH to Sarah, 29 August 1870, HIL
6. Paris is in a state of terrible excitement. All foreigners are hurrying out of it, IH to Sarah, 31 August 1870, HIL
7. When the Germans first arrived, the Marie was anxious to assist their labours by quartering their men on the town, Messrs Holden and Son's Manufactory at Rheims, September 20 1870, *Leeds Mercury*
8. to try to get money to tide over our difficulties, Jonathan Holden to Angus Holden, 15 September 1870, HIL
9. When I tell you that he pays some seven or eight hundred pounds every week in wages, A Yorkshire manufacturer at Rheims, 23 September 1870, *The Hull Packet and East Riding Time.*
10. there is great distress in Roubaix, Isaac Crothers to IH, 26 September 1870, HIL
11. We are still working night and day, Isaac Crothers to IH, 7 October 1870, HIL
12. saw the frightful traces of war, IH to Sarah, November 1 1870, HIL
13. I had gone into the deplorable state of the present strife too fully. November 8 1870, Jonathan Holden to Angus Holden, HIL
14. 3 days a week, Isaac Crothers to IH, November 11 1870, HIL
15. The *franc tireurs* continue to give much trouble to the German troops, Jonathan Holden to IH, 14 November 1870, HIL

16. entire families with little children, fleeing from Amiens, Jonathan Holden to Angus Holden, December 10 1870, HIL

17. in the future the two peoples will see their true interest otherwise than in the deadly strife, Jonathan Holden to Angus Holden, December 14 1870, HIL

18. All our railways are still entirely in their hands, Jonathan Holden to Isaac Crothers, 6 March 1871, Bundle 3/1/3 JBPL

19. After what has passed during the last two months …you may well feel anxious about the present and ultimate position of poor unfortunate France, Jonathan Holden to Isaac Crothers, 2 June 1871, Bundle 3/1/3, JBPL

20. Estimate profits for the year ending 30 June 1871 at f 359,859.25, so that "Glory' has cost us a round million, Jonathan Holden to Isaac Holden, 27 July 1871, Bundle 3/1/3, JBPL

Chapter 11.

1. no orator. My work has not been to make sentences, 24 January 1872, *Leeds Mercury*

2. against the drink habits of this unenlightened 19th Century, BL

3. Though he seems to be an attractive speaker on the stump, he never that I recollect spoke in the House, September 14 1872, *The Graphic*,

4. a supporter of godless education, 14 February 1874, *Huddersfield Chronicle*

5. How can you support such a rabid Nonconformist? 9 February 1974, *York Herald*

6. to distinguish between faithful servants and those who had lost that character, Alfred Illingworth reported 28 January 1874, *Bradford Observer*,

7. the bulk of employers had conceded one hour on Saturdays, August 4 1872, *Reynolds Newspaper*

8. it would be our ruin – at least until the Germans and the French, our greatest competitors, reduce their hours, Isaac Holden speaking 13 May 1892 to the *Bradford Observer*

9. Employers, he thought, do very foolishly in refusing to accept the intelligent picked men of the various trades as deputations or representatives, Isaac Holden speaking 13 May 1892 to the *Bradford Observer*

10. negotiations over wages and other aspects of working conditions were quickly completed, Technology and Enterprise, Honeyman and Goodman.

11. the bulk of employers had conceded one hour on Saturdays, making a weeks work 59 instead of 60, Captain Shepherd, July 30 1872, *Daily News*

12. it would be our ruin – at least until the Germans and the French, our greatest competitors, reduce their hours, 13 May 1892, *Bradford Observer*,

13. There were the same beautiful machines that I had seen in operation at the Alston Works at Bradford but the workers were altogether different, June 1875 *Bradford Observer*

14. The handmill gives you society with the feudal lord, the steam mill society with the industrial capitalist, *The Poverty of Philosophy*, Karl Marx, 1847

15. The richest man, probably in the British House of Commons is Mr Isaac Holden, , 24 January 1889, *New York Tribune*

16. had not given a valuable machine to the wool trade, 10 June 1875, *Leeds Mercury*

17. prejudiced either by interest, vanity, or caprice, 10 June 1875, *Leeds Mercury*

18. surprise and regret at Mr. Holden's long and angry letter, 17 June 1875, *Leeds Mercury*

19. an ingenious, hard-working, self-made inventor, 8 July 1875, *Leeds Mercury*

20. Mr. Lister is the victim of an ungovernable jealousy, 19 August 1875, *Leeds Mercury*

21. the awful offence of being represented in the catalogue of the Royal Academy as "the inventor of the combing machine", 31 July 1875, *Bradford Observer*,

22. were few men so conspicuous as to deserve them, and those who deserved them most certainly required them the least, 27 July 1877, John Bright, *Newcastle Courant*,

23. I have no inclination to continue this useless and disagreeable correspondence, Jonathan Holden to Isaac Crothers, 17 March 1875, Bundle 1/1/3, JBPL

24. I must have each concern working at the top of its capital and will use all the means for doing so without friction, Isaac Holden to Jonathon Holden and Isaac Crothers, December 1878, Bundle 1/3/5 JBPL

25. I fear we shall have to break with Jonathon, Isaac Holden to Sarah, 23 January 1880, Bundle 1/2/19 JBPL

26. We spent yesterday visiting several of our customers and we found Jonathan is condemned by them, Isaac to Sarah, 1 July 1880, HIL

27. This is a crafty bid for popularity – worthy of its author, Angus Holden to IH, 26 May 1887, Bundle 3/1/5 JBPL

28. For the last 9 years, for reasons of your own, you have chosen to ignore me and mine, John Edward Holden to Isaac, 30 March 1889, Box 9, BL

Chapter 12.

1. not a word which has fallen from him should in the slightest degree lessen your regard for him, Alfred Illingworth reported 8 December 1882 in the *Bradford Observer*

2. Justice and conciliation, 15 May 1883, *Leeds Mercury*

3. Vote for Holden and the Land League, 18 May 1882, *Leeds Mercury,*

4. The great majority has cheered me and made me thankful, Lady Frederick Cavendish to IH, May 18 1882, HIL

207

5. if his death were to work good to his fellow-men, which indeed was the whole object of his life, Obituary – Lady Frederick Cavendish, 23 April 1875, *The Times*

6. As soon as I had taken the oath Mr. Gladstone, Mr. Bright and others of the Ministers gave me a hearty shake of the hand, IH to Sarah Holden, May 23 1875, HIL

7. sense of duty (which) supports me in being deprived of these dear pleasures, November 7 1882, IH to Sarah Holden, HIL

8. I only wish I could go for the air and walks (at Oakworth) but also that I might have you in my arms every night, IH to Sarah, 17 July 1882, Bundle 1/2/20 JBPL

9. cordial support to the "Grand Old Man". November 7 1882, IH to Sarah Holden, HIL

10. When I see Mr. Gladstone always at his weary work sitting by the Table, November 7 1882, IH to Sarah Holden, HIL

11. Indeed, there was reason to believe that Charles Bradlaugh had himself materially modified his views before his death, October 1893, *The Freethinker*

12. One of the smallest men in the House of Commons; and he is slight and thin. A peculiar feature of Mr. Holden is the brilliance of his eyes. 19 November 1888, *The Star*

13. Quakers…spoke of their liberality to Methodists, IH to Sarah 14 July 1882, Bundle 1/2/20 JBPL

14. send me my court dress and sword, IH to Sarah, 25 March 1883 Bundle 1/2/1 JBPL

15. at 80 degrees temperature in which I use a soap lather to cleanse the skin thoroughly with friction, IH to Mrs Gladstone, December 27 1884, HIL

16. The hereditary principle is out of harmony with the spirit of the age, Angus Holden election address to the Electors of the East Riding, 21 October 1885, Bundle 1/3/3 JBPL

17. In consequence of the resignation of the Government I shall come down tomorrow, IH to Sarah, June 9th 1885, Bundle 1/2/24 JBPL

18. Mr. Lucy says there will be no difficulty in distinguishing between you two in the House of Commons, Annie Lucy to IH, December 1, 1885, HIL

19. The beautiful diamonds you gave us were all duly worn and were quite worth the occasion. Margaret Illingworth to IH, May 17 1888, HIL

20. into the House to hear Parnell's very able speech… delivered in his usual calm but effective style, IH to Sarah, August 25th 1886, Bundle 1/1/23 JBPL

21. I think it would have been rum if I had not come up to support Parnell, February 21st 1887, Bundle 1/1/23 JBPL

Chapter 13.

1. unusually large salaries, IH to John Metcalfe, 10 November 1888. Bundle 4/2/6, JPBL

2. that of keeping the place at the top of the tree, John Metcalfe to IH, 14 November 1888, Bundle 4/2/6 JBPL

3. I have a distinct recollection of having originated all the improvements you name, IH to John Metcalfe, 19 January 1889, Bundle 4/2/6 JBPL

4. The claim put forward by Mr. Holden of having suggested the Square Motion was not borne out by the facts contained in his letter written at that time, James Burnley to IH, undated (circa September 1888), Bundle 1/4/12 JBPL

5. I have had a sort of mist thrown over me out of which I should have been glad of your guidance, James Burnley to IH, 22 December 1886, Bundle 1/4/14, JBPL

6. does not amount to much, IH to Burnley , 30 March 1887, Bundle 1/4/14, JBPL

7. for permission to refer to his private, Retrospective Notes on Wool-combing, Preface to James Burnley, The History of Wool and Wool-Combing, 1891

8. Who made the combing of fine wool, practical by machinery; and who made it a great commercial success "IT WAS I THAT DID AND I ALONE.' S.C. Lister to Donnisthorpe Jnr, 12 November 1888, Bundle 1/4/14, JBPL

9. who never ceased to contend that I had done him less than justice, James Burnley's Literary Recollections 1870-1890, cited in J.M. Trickett's, Technological appraisal of the Isaac Holden Papers

10. I find that such Patent contains the first patented embodiment of the principle of the "Square Motion" invention', James Burnley letter to Lord Masham, published in Lister. S.C., Lord Masham's Inventions, 1905

11. The West Lancashire Railway is not doing as well as we would like on account on the smallpox epidemic at Preston, Edward Holden to IH, August 28 1888, Bundle 3/1/5 JBPL

12. I am overwhelmed with grief. I will not run away from it whatever happens, Edward Holden to IH, March 23 1889, Box 9, BL

13. The public are having confidence in us. Our shares can not be had, no one will part with what they hold, Edward Holden to IH, September 6 1889, Bundle 3/1/5 JBPL

14. so it appears he has ample income for his requirements without drawing from the business, Angus Holden to IH, July 12 1889, Box 9, BL

Chapter 14.

1. Mr. Isaac Holden, M.P on Health and Longevity, 1982, Bundle 5/4, JBPL

2. Had she only followed strictly my deictic rules, she would still be alive. Character Sketch of Sir Isaac Holden, Emily Crawford published in the Review of Reviews. Bundle 5/7 JBPL

3. for obtaining Letters Patent under the Great Seal conferring upon you the Dignity of a Baronetcy of the United Kingdom, Home Department to IH, 27 June 1893, Bundle 11/1/29 JBPL

4. The free importation of foreign goods, and that Free Trade is the cause of all our loss and trouble, lecture by Samuel Lister entitled, England's

Folly, at the Silk Section of the Jubilee Exhibition in Manchester on October 21st 1887.

5. That they have earned in the past not only good wages but very good wages, is certain, or the Manningham ladies, the 'plushers', as they are called could not dress in the way they do, Letter from SC Lister, December 26th 1890, *Bradford Observer*

6. They paraded the streets with bayonets drawn and charged the people in various directions, 13 April 1890, *The Times*,

7. at least as good a Nonconformist as Mr. Alfred Illingworth, June 14 1892, *Leeds Mercury*

8. If you persist in opposing the Labour Movement ... we shall establish our own Labour Church, Socialism Over Sixty Years: The Life of Jowett in Bradford 1864 – 1944, Fenner Brockway, London 1946

9. References to Ben Tillett are taken from the biography of Ben Tillett by Jonathan Schneer, Croom and Helm, 1982

10. A sturdy, old fashioned individualist, Sidney Webb, "The Moral of the Elections", August 1892, *Contemporary Review* page 273.

11. in 1894 Illingworth argued that mill-girls should do one third more work for the same pay, 30 June 1894, *Labour Leader* page 5

12. I do not object to Mr. Ben Tillett, or Mr. Ker Hardie, or any one else looking forward to the millennium, Fifty Years of Politics, Mr. Alfred Illingworth's Retrospective, 1905

Chapter 15.

1. It would be our ruin – at least until the Germans and the French, our great competitors, reduced their hours, May 1892, *Bradford Observer*

2. Illingworthism is a gospel without sympathy, comradeship, or hope for the Bradford worker, *Daily Chronicle* - quoted in the *Labour Leader* 21 November 1896

3. Monomaniacal Gladstonian, 1 February 1894, *Methodist Times*

4. A rather unlooked for, but very welcome appearance in last night's debate on the Budget Bill was that of Sir Isaac Holden, 11 May 1894, *Daily Chronicle* editorial

5. I shall always remember that nothing did more to secure the passing of the Budget than the admirable speech, Sir William Harcourt to Isaac Holden 4 August 1894

6. As a young man he heartily joined in the agitation for Catholic emancipation, and for the great Reform Bill of 1832, July 20 1895, *Keighley Daily News*

7. the animus of my pubic life in politics – rights, liberty and independence, Isaac Holden's Notes, Bundle 1/1/29, JBPL.

8. Instead of bequeathing to my sons equal portions of my estate I by this codicil bequeath to each of my daughters Mary and Margaret double. Codicil to Isaac Holden's Will 1896, BL

9. she is rich intelligent and kind hearted. She is quite able, if only we could stir her up to the point, to do great things financially for the women's cause, cited in Women's Suffrage Movement by Elizabeth Crawford, source Elizabeth Wolstenholme Elmy papers, British Library

10. to the end the same gentle, modest, sympathetic man, there was summer always about him, Mr. Christian's funeral oration Oakworth chapel, HIL

11. Sir, At last that wonderful man, Sir Isaac Holden, has joined the great majority, and the story of his life is now before the public, 2nd September 1897, letter from Lister to the Editor of *The Engineer*

12. Although Lord Masham's outrageous letter put him outside the pale of courteous argument, Wordsworth Donnisthorpe, 28 September 1897, to the Editor of the *Yorkshire Post* (published on 30 September)

Index

A

Edward Ackroyd 106
J. Adams-Acton 79
Anti-Corn law League 19
Betty Ackroyd 23, 193
James Ambler 25
Alston Works 62, 72–74, 87, 138, 140, 206
Sir William Armstrong 81, 160

B

Jeremy Bentham 105
Count Bismark 129
Fenner Brockway 173, 190, 211
Robbie Burns 10–11
Butterfield 13
Bradford 5, 7–8, 17, 21–22, 24, 26–27, 29–31, 33, 37, 48, 52, 55–56, 61–62, 65–66, 68, 70–72, 75–78, 81, 87, 93, 102–103, 106–107, 117–118, 120, 124, 131, 134, 136, 138–141, 143–144, 147–149, 156–157, 166, 168, 170–174, 177–178, 183–184, 186, 188–190, 192–194, 199, 203, 205–207, 211
Bradford Woolcombers Report 190
John Bright 9, 19, 72, 79–80, 111, 115, 119, 144, 154, 157, 170, 200, 202, 207
James Burnley 73, 91, 160, 199, 209–210
Burne-Jones 81
Charles Bradlaugh 151–152, 208

C

Lord Frederick Cavendish 119, 135, 150
Lady Cavendish 150
Joseph Chamberlain 149
Thomas Craig 73, 86
William Craven 47, 195
Collier 18, 21
Collett 55–58
Tom Collins 108–110
Richard Cobden 18–19, 70
Isaac Holden Crothers 42, 51, 60, 145
Cullingworth 15, 17, 20, 29, 40, 168
Chartists 19
Croix 51, 54, 60, 62–63, 71, 87, 102, 127, 130–131, 139–140, 144–145, 159

213

Crofts 65–67, 186
John Crossley 108

D

George Edmund Donnisthorpe 25
Wordsworth Donnisthorpe 186, 212
Disraeli 113, 121

E

Earl of Dartmouth 13
Eastbrook 29, 31, 68, 102, 200

F

John Fraser 10, 19, 192
Baron de Fourment 27, 48, 67
Charles Faulkner 60
Mary Faulkner 60
W.E. Forster 9, 61, 118, 122–123, 136, 141, 148–149, 190, 203

G

Gambetta 127, 131
Tamar Gill 147
Gladstone 9, 79, 107, 111, 113–116, 118–119, 123, 150–151, 155–158, 169, 176, 182, 190, 203, 208
Glasgow 15
Jordan Goodman 27, 189, 194
Gomersal 43

H

Kier Hardie 9, 174, 180

William Harcourt 176–179, 212
Angus Holden 53, 75–76, 81, 86, 94–95, 116, 118, 130, 146, 157, 159, 176–177, 186–187, 197–200, 202–205, 207–208, 210
Edward Holden 9, 77, 82, 86, 96, 163, 188, 207, 210
Sir Edward Holden 9, 82, 188
John Edward Holden 207
Mary Holden 75, 99, 145, 195
Jonathan Holden 9, 42, 51, 61, 63–64, 97–98, 125, 129, 133, 142, 144, 146–147, 161–162, 185, 197–198, 204–205, 207
Katrina Honeyman 27, 189, 194

I

Albert Holden Illingworth 145
Daniel Illingworth 75
Eustace Illingworth 29, 188
Henry Illingworth 75–76, 99, 145, 159, 200
Alfred Illingworth 9, 77, 100, 106, 117–118, 123, 136, 138, 148, 157, 172–174, 177, 183, 205, 207, 211
Margaret Illingworth 77, 209
Francis Holden Illingworth 82
Percy Illingworth 184

J

Johnstone 10, 12
Samuel Jones 14

K

Knaresborough 107–109, 111–113, 117, 136, 202

John Kennedy 12, 16–17, 193
Keighley 71, 117, 121, 150, 153, 156–157, 166, 176–178, 181, 184, 189, 212
Robert Kell 78, 106

L

John Lewthwaite 146
Marion Love 12
Angus Love 16, 78, 200
Robert Lowe 111
Leeds 5, 8, 12–13, 17, 24, 78, 107, 127, 142, 150, 155, 188–189, 192, 201, 203–207, 211
Ellis Cunliffe Lister 24
Samuel Cunliffe Lister 7, 9, 21, 24, 93, 169
Lucifer match 14–15, 142
Sir Francis Lycett 104, 201
Sir Henry Lucy 156

M

Manningham 24–25, 50, 67, 141, 170–172, 174, 211
Manningham Mills 170, 172
Metcalfe 60, 159–160, 209
John Stuart Mill 115
John Morley 9, 116, 157, 176, 203
A.J. Mundella 72, 137
Edward Miall 9, 106, 114, 117, 190, 203

N

Nenthead 11
Louis Napoleon 28, 49–50, 64
Noble 55, 65, 129

O

Captain O'Shea 149
Oakworth 9, 29, 46, 78–81, 102, 141, 151, 155, 166, 168, 182, 184, 208, 212
Overall 60, 156
William Outhwaite 62

P

Palmer 155
Parnell 149–150, 156–158, 209
Tom Paine 10
Paisley 10, 12, 14, 16, 21, 192
Pit Lane 21, 56
Paris 18, 26–28, 31–33, 41–42, 45–46, 48–49, 64–65, 68, 71, 76, 79, 125, 127, 129, 131–132, 146, 166, 196, 200–201, 204
Miss Pickles 44, 166
Powell 135

R

Sir John Ramsden 136
Reform Club 154, 158
Henry Ripley 18, 118, 134, 137, 148
Reims 61–65, 71, 102, 125, 127–129, 131–132, 139–140, 144–147, 159, 197
John Ruskin 103

S

Charles Sauria 14
Schlumberger 51–52
Captain Shepherd 137, 206
Slaithwaite 13

Sigston 13
Sarah Sugden 9, 29, 85, 147, 194
Jonas Sugden 48, 54, 195–197, 200–201
James Sugden 65
Mary Susannah Sugden 147
St Denis 41, 44, 46, 48, 53–55, 57, 60, 63, 71, 76, 102, 189
Adam Smith 137
George Smith 78
Swire Smith 121

T

Ben Tillett 172, 174, 190, 211
Titus Salt 61, 107, 118, 137
Titus Salt Junior 118
Townsends 15, 17–18, 20–21, 26
Edward Townsend 40
Eliza Townsend 42, 44
Robert Townsend 17, 20–21
Trevelyan 111
Trickett 58, 210

W

John Walker 15
Waddy 20
Watts 43–44, 195
Sidney Webb 173–174, 211
Women's Suffrage 183, 212
Basil Wood 108
Maria Wood 77